Dedications and ack

I dedicate this book to all those

countries when they could take no more of danger, adversity and hardship and took to the road to freedom.

To those who left a life behind and forged a new life in a new land.

To those who had to prove their worth time and again and have succeeded to overcome prejudice, isolation and discrimination.

To all the people working in the NHS, wherever they come from

My thanks go to my supportive family, especially to my grandchildren, who through asking questions about my life spurred me into writing.

Heart felt thanks to my teacher, friend and tutor Claudia Gould, to my friend- writer and editor- Anna Rahman for all the advice and help with spelling and grammar and continuous encouragement.

MiryVicks

IMMIGRATION MASTERCLASS

By Miry Vicks

First published in the UK in 2015 by CompletelyNovel.com

ISBN Number 9781849148221

Printed in the UK by Lightning Source International

1
THE PASSPORT

'The passport is here; it arrived this morning by post!' George holds it in his hand for me to see, as he opens the door to greet me. He is so excited that he does not even make room for me to enter the house.

I look at the green covers with shiny gold letters: *Socialist Republic of Romania*. And underneath that the magic word: *Passport*. I open it at the last page and a younger me is staring back at me from the photo taken a good few years before. My hair was short then and my face carefully made up. It was before I had my daughter.

I feel nothing. I've waited for it so long with a mixture of hope and dread that now, when it is here in George's hand, I am inert. My emotions are all spent. George is my husband's father. He is the one who has a say in everything we do. Sometimes I like it and other times I don't. More often than not I believe in what he stands for. All his life was spent fighting for his country to be free, and he and the whole family suffered grave consequences as a result. The hope that all of us will escape from the regime of terror is the only thing that keeps him alive.

The year is 1968 and the relationship between Romania and Israel has slightly improved. Ceausescou, the Romanian president, has agreed to allow Romanian Jews to visit their families in Israel. Eight years ago I applied for a visa to visit my family and only now I received an answer. My husband is behind my father-in-law and our eyes meet. Dan's eyes are alight with new hope. George's elderly cheeks are moist with tears, and joy begins to rise in me; this time it's for real. Not like a few months before, when a letter arrived stating that my application for a visa to visit my family overseas had been approved. The next day, full of enthusiasm, I went back to the hospital where I had been working for the last six years and told my news to whoever wanted to listen. Rocco, Eugene and Elena congratulated me. They were my colleagues; they were my friends. I even plucked up enough courage to tell Marius but he said nothing. My friends whispered in my ear, 'If, by any chance, you decide not to come back, good luck and don't forget to send me an invitation.'

'But of course I will come back. It's only a month's holiday,' I always replied.

'Well, if I were you, I would do what most people do when they get out of this country: abscond and never look back.'

I denied emphatically that I would do such a thing, but I knew what they were all thinking. So many people fled: mostly educated, professional people – even the ones in high, solid positions such as party members, international sportsmen and musicians. Each time the opportunity arose, one or two escaped from the supervision of the security person attached to their group and stayed behind in the free country that they were visiting. They left partners and children behind and all their possessions, which, at a later date, would be confiscated by the 'state power'.

A few days afterwards another letter arrived, advising me to ignore the previous one; the decision was annulled and I was invited, together with my husband, to attend a meeting at the Department of Foreign Affairs. It was obvious to me: one of the people I had shared my good news with had informed the secret services of my upcoming departure and most probably expressed some doubts about my return. The atmosphere at home changed into one of quiet reproach, the unseen finger pointing at me.

The day of the meeting arrived. We were both questioned and, with my best air of sincerity, I assured the three officials looking sternly at me that I had no intention of deserting, as I had my little daughter, my husband, and my parents and sister to return to after the holiday. I left, unsure as to whether I had been believed, but I was told that the application would be reconsidered at the next panel meeting. Deep in my soul I did not even believe myself in what I had said. I am not good at making decisions; to be perfectly honest, I prefer to have decisions taken out of my hands by fate or events. Perhaps it was meant not to happen.

Months went by, and I was reconciled, even hoping that I would be refused. I could not see myself parting from my daughter, although I saw very little of Nicky. Her grandparents cared for her. I left home early each morning, long before she was awake, and I was back well after her bedtime. The hospital where I was working was 60 kilometres from the capital and I was commuting there daily. The slow train took two to three hours each way. Although Nicky and I spent so little time together, she was mine and I loved her dearly. I was still living in hope that one day I might pass the competition and be given a place of work in Bucharest.

Also, I was increasingly attracted to one of my colleagues, a fellow commuter, and that frightened me. I wanted to spend all my time with Marius, listen to his words, absorb his wit and feel the touch of his skin on mine. He was not particularly good-looking but he was attractive and exuded sex appeal. I knew, when I dared to think about it, that there was no future in the relationship; neither of us would destroy our own families for a desperate commuters' romance. If I went abroad and never came back, given time, all that would end; the attraction would fade and the desire would subside.

And now here it is: the green, shiny passport greets me at the door. As it is such a rare event for someone to own a passport in 1960s Romania, I have to treasure the moment, in the knowledge that this passport will be taken away from me on my return. If I return…

I look at George. His hope of leaving the country he fought for - the country he came back to help rebuild, but which made him suffer physical and mental humiliation - is rekindled. I turn to look at Dan, my husband for the last seven years. He smiles politely, betraying nothing. I sometimes wonder if there is anything behind that smile. He never voices an opinion; he avoids confrontation or discussions, anything that 'rocks the boat'. He is a good father; he loves Nicky dearly but when it comes to caring for her, he is an expert at manipulating his parents or sisters to do the job. That is why he has repeatedly refused to apply to obtain a place of our own. He finds it more convenient to live with his parents, all five of us, in an apartment built for two. He stands there behind his father, and I catch him looking at my passport with pleasure, grinning like a cat when it spots a saucer of cream.

I walk in and look for my Nicky, who is already tucked up in bed in the little back room. Her hair covers half of her face. The fading light coming through the window as the night approaches sets sparkles of gold in her hair. I part it gently and kiss her forehead. Her eyes open and her face breaks into a smile. Obviously, she was only pretending to sleep.

'Mummy, Mummy be quiet!' she whispers. 'The kitty is sleeping!' Indeed I notice, curled up at the end of the bed, the black-and-white cat that I gave her. But I left strict instructions that the cat should not be allowed in her bed because the other day I noticed fleabites on Nicky's arms and legs. I do not have the heart to chase the cat out because then Nicky will not sleep, so I close her eyes with kisses and slowly move out of the room.

In the dining room the two men are sitting round the table, their faces set like we are going to have a serious meeting. My mother-in-law is away visiting her younger daughter, Amy. The men will have to wait. The mirror on the dining room wall catches my reflection: I look pale; my hair is dull and unruly, and I have bags under my eyes. I look smaller. I note with pleasure that I have lost weight. I go to the bathroom to take a shower. The water is cold but on this hot August evening I don't mind. It was different during winter. I cannot think of anything; my head is full of the news.

I have a passport. I can fly outside the cage, even if only for a short while. I return to the dining room refreshed to face the two men. It is George who starts talking: 'I hope you've learned your lesson. Nobody must hear of this till the day after you've left.'

'All right!' I say, a bit annoyed at being reminded.

'You must not worry; we'll manage,' Dan says.

Then it dawns on me: my mother-in-law is away, so who is going to look after my little girl? My mother? Unlikely. Both my parents work long hours and were against my going abroad from the start. They have never considered emigrating, no matter what hardship they endured. Not before my sister Bea had got her degree.

'We'll hire a nanny and Nicky's at the nursery during the day. Pappy will be going to collect her from there, as he already does, and he will spend time with her till Lydia comes back from work.' Dan seems to have it all sorted out. He lowers his eyes and starts collecting breadcrumbs from the table, kneading them into small bread balls. George takes what I call his leader posture: his chest thrust forward, his head lifted a fraction. He closes one eye and lifts his right hand. For a second, with his moustache, he reminds me of someone.

'I think we have agreed on a plan: you will not come back till you have tried all avenues, explored all possibilities and met all the people who are likely to get us all out of here,' he whispers. It is hard to understand him above the sound of running water from the bathroom, which is our safety measure against being overheard.

'Yes,' I say, not very convincingly, 'of course.' *Yes,* I think, *I agreed long ago to be the family's passport to freedom.* That was before I had a child - before I understood what it is to be a mother. Dan says nothing.

I am beginning to curse this green passport. It would have been better if it had never arrived. I have to decide and I hate making decisions. But I do not have to decide now, this evening, so I say, 'Yes' to everything and in my mind I feel I will be away for three weeks on a holiday to see the family I have never met. It will be the first time I visit a country other than my own. Night is making itself known. It is time for bed and tomorrow I will have to wake up early to catch my train. If I miss it, the next train will be at midday and I will be in trouble again. I take my passport and put it on my bedside table; its green cover turns black with the advancing darkness. Dan gets into bed, still saying nothing, and I turn to sleep but he wants to make love. I do not feel like it. In the end I give in; we make love quietly and then go to sleep.

The next day and the following ones go by with the speed of a dream. I go to work and I come back, bursting with worries and emotions, and I have no one to talk to - not even Marius. I see my patients and speak with them but I do not pay attention. My mind is stuck like a broken record: will I go or will I not? In my spare time I meet and interview a few women recommended to me for the nanny job - just in case I do go, as I have promised.

Dan says, 'It's up to you.'

The following weekend I take the train to see my parents. 'It is your decision,' my mother's resigned look meets my eyes.

'Great! That's what I want to hear!' I mutter to myself.

My father is more encouraging. 'Take the chance,' he says. 'It may not come again. At least go and see for yourself what it is like.'

I wish I could confide in Marius but I am too frightened. His wise words would be such a comfort. But who knows who betrayed me? I will have to leave without even saying goodbye.

Back home, intense preparations are taking place. George asks a close friend of his to make a microphotocopy of his War Service certificate, stating his contribution to the liberation of Europe. I have to carry this with me, hidden deep on my person. I will also carry a photograph showing my father-in-law with Dan as a child on his lap, together with five other men. They are the group of Free Romanian Journalists who operated in Palestine under the command of the British Allied forces. The photo is small and George has inscribed on the back, in tiny letters, their names and last address known to him for each of them. George wants me to search for them during my stay and, if I find them, tell them about our predicament and ask for their help.

I think I can do that. *I will do it.* Then I will come back. Yes, this will give me time to think, cool down from my hopeless thoughts, see new things and escape the dreary commuting to a provincial no-hope hospital. I will escape the well-meaning but patronising in-laws, and perhaps manage to bring out my Nicky and my husband, so we can start afresh on our own, like a real family. The virus of freedom digs deep and spreads.

The day of my departure becomes, finally, an immediate reality: tomorrow at midday. My sister Bea comes to spend the night with us. Aurora and Nelly - two of my closest friends -come to see me and I cannot hold back anymore; I tell them my news, and I assure them that I will be back and we will spend Christmas together. I can't tell Dan or his parents how I feel but a conviction grows stronger in me and I know that I could not be separated from Nicky - not a month, not even for a few days. After my friends leave, I go to see Nicky and kiss her goodnight; I hold her tight. She is giggling, saying that I am tickling her. In secrecy, I pack in what would be my hand luggage a few of her belongings, enough to see us through a few days - just in case.

The next day becomes today and, early in the morning, the long journey by taxi to Otopeni Airport has started. I wear the light-blue ski pants which I had bought from an elderly Jewish neighbour who receives monthly parcels from her family in Canada. She sells the contents to supplement her income. Dan also bought from her for me a quilted dressing gown with a large floral pattern, the likes of which we had never seen before here. I carefully packed it, together with some lead cut glass vases: presents for my host family. In the suitcase I added a nightdress, summer dresses, another pair of shoes and, hidden in the double lining, my stethoscope, to avoid rising suspicion about my intentions.

I have the green and gold passport in my bag and the micro-photos hidden deep near my breast. I have never been in the airport. It is of recent construction, all glass and concrete, and a sea of people are moving to and fro. A uniformed officer asks to see my passport. I hand it to him, still hoping that he will say: 'No, go back home,' but he hands it back without even looking at me. The whole family is there: Dan, George, my sister Bea, Dan's sister and her husband. It is early and we spend a couple of hours standing and talking. Finally, the chain is lifted, and officials in uniform and an armed soldier signal to us to come through. Crowds of people surge forward. George takes Nicky by the hand and invites her to go to the kiosk where they sell ice cream. The two of them disappear into the crowd. I cannot even say goodbye to her. It is better that way. I keep calm: I know what I have to do. I hug and kiss each one of my relatives, and then I kiss Dan. His eyes are moist. 'Don't forget. Do what you can; we are all behind you,' he whispers, and we kiss goodbye again. He turns to leave and I stay in the long queue to check in.

I catch glimpses of Nicky on the other side of the corridor near the kiosk. I push through and break away from my place in the queue until I reach her. George is stuck in the crowd at the ice cream kiosk. His back is turned and his raised hand waves money. I grab Nicky's hand and drag her along to the exit.

'Mummy, my ice cream!' she wails.

'Never mind! I will buy you another one as soon as we're out of here.'

She is in tears, looking back. I hold on tight. We finally get through and I wave for a taxi. I bundle in a bewildered Nicky and climb in myself.

'Quick,' I say, 'to the North Train Station!'

I haven't thought out a plan but I will. Perhaps I will take the train to the town where my hospital is. I'll find rooms and a nanny. Or I'll go to my parents first and spend my holiday there.

But of course, I don't do any of this. That is not what happened. Instead, I inched forward with the crowd, till my turn came. Then I turned my head towards Dan and the family, who were still waving, and went through the departure gate.

I still sometimes wonder what life would have been like if…

The bug of freedom was already deep-seated in my brain; that impulse of leaving the country and the misery behind, no matter at what cost, was stronger. I followed the crowd through the departure gate and I lost sight of my people.

2
TAROM

The plane is large and more spacious than I had imagined. My seat is by the window and next to me is an empty seat. Not all the seats are taken, and I am not surprised. Not many Romanians travel abroad these days. From time to time I touch my chest where, deep inside my bra, are the photo and the copy of George's certificate. I have to make sure for the zillionth time that they are still there. The flight attendants are busy closing the overhead lockers. She is a lovely, young, blonde woman and he is a dark, slim man. When he turns round, to my surprise, I recognise him. He is Vladimir, a boy I knew years ago, when he was a child. He lived in the same building as us and was a skinny, shy boy who could not speak well. His mother used to call me to examine him each time he had an earache. Poor chap, he suffered so much with his ears! He could not hear well at times and he was slow to speak. He was small for his age and withdrawn, unlike his eldest brother who was very sporty, tall and good-looking. I recall how Vladimir used to abscond from school - but look at him now! A steward on an international flight! How did he get the job? Obviously, through the right connections.

When they moved into the third-floor flat, we became wary of that family; it was rumoured that the father and mother were staunch Communists and supporters of the regime, just like the other family across the landing, who moved in almost at the same time. We even laughed at the fact that both families gave Russian first names to their younger children: Vladimir and Tamara. In time, they proved to be quite friendly and although we kept our distance, we were on good terms with those neighbours. I visited them more often than the other members of my family, due to Vladimir's frequent spells of illness. But as time passed and he grew up, I visited less and less, and in the end I lost touch.

He recognises me as well and for a short while it is awkward for both of us. He looks furtively left and right, making sure that none of his colleagues is watching; after all, contact with someone going to Israel may raise suspicions. I feel uneasy as well, in case he asks questions and reports further to someone in authority. However, we find a moment to greet each other and exchange news. Vladimir tells me that his brother, who is in the national basketball team, is allowed to travel to most counties and is engaged to be married. After that, Vladimir returns to his duties and I return to my troubled thoughts. In my mind's eye I see my Nicky playing 'married' with the other three kids living in the neighbourhood. Nicky is in charge; she shares out the parts and determines the position that each child has to take. And of course, she is always the happy bride, little Bobby is the groom and Daniela always remains the bridesmaid, to her great discontent. After all, she wants to get married as well. But the children do whatever Nicky tells them to do. She is a born leader. I smile to myself until my reverie is interrupted by the arrival of a meal on a tray. I excuse myself, saying that I am not hungry. Vladimir passes by and whispers, 'Eat, Doctor' – he still calls me that – 'it is included in the price of the flight!' And I gratefully tuck in. After that I close my eyes again but my troubled mind does not let me rest. I see Vladimir again a little later as he pushes a trolley together with his colleague, the blonde stewardess. On the trolley are wonderful things: cigarettes, chocolate and perfume in splendid bottles. I hear people around me asking for the prices: $20 for this, $40 for that; they do not take Romanian currency. There is no point in my asking; I have no dollars. I have never seen a dollar.

I return to my reveries. I see Dan, walking up the path back from work. I know it is him by the uneven step on the paving stones; he keeps saying that his left leg is shorter than his right. He comes in and smiles his weak smile. He takes off his hat and loosens his tie, says hello to everyone and then sits down to eat. Before that, though, he grabs the daily newspaper from the desk, props it up against his glass, and starts reading the headlines and eating at the same time. How many times have I told him that it is not good for him to do that? It is unhealthy! But he takes no notice. There is no conversation during the meal, as both Dan and George have their nose buried deep into their newspaper. Silky and I busy ourselves in the kitchen or go to read Nicky a little bedtime story. After a time I rejoin the others and I start talking of my daily news, my journey, what the hospital surgeon said - nothing special, just chat. Dan, still with his nose in the paper, just grunts from time to time to give the impression that he is listening, but I know he is not and my voice trails away. Then it is time for the news bulletin; we have a black and white television. The first programme starts at 7 o'clock with the news, which is mostly dominated by what the president did and where he went. This is followed by news from the Soviet Union; some achievements of the workforce, who was nominated for the best tractor driver in the land, the success of the five-year plan… the usual rubbish. Then we pile up in the bathroom with the radio and the running water to listen to the other news: Radio Free Europe, Call Israel, and so on. I go to bed early, as the next morning I will wake up at 4 o'clock. I am the first up; George wakes up as well and goes into the kitchen to make sandwiches for me and Dan. It is his duty. He will go back to bed later, after he has seen us all off to work. I gratefully grab the cup of coffee he has made and rush through the door.

Then I wonder: where is the Dan I used to know? I see us coming out of the Albatros, the restaurant by the lake where we went dancing with our friends. Dan walks with his coat pockets bulging on each side, my stiletto heels sticking out, and I, in my party dress set on numerous petticoats, walk beside him barefoot. We laugh and joke happily. Seven years have passed since then. We have both changed. Perhaps it is a good thing for us to take a break from each other, to get time to see where we stand.

3
REUNION

The TAROM flight lands at Lod Airport . I am tense and full of apprehension; will anybody come to greet me? What if they have not had the telegram? Will I recognise Abraham - my mother's brother - and his wife? They are the ones who invited me. I have no recollection of them, although my mother said that I met them when I was little. All I know about them is what I have gathered from the photos taken at their wedding in my mother's album and from what my mother has told me. They were childhood sweethearts; he was about 21 and had just completed his military service and she was about 17. They had met at the Maccabbi club frequented by young Jews interested in sports. As the war was threatening and anti-Semitism was rising, they took heed and left for Palestine.

I descend the steps and a wall of hot air hits me in the face. I must have stepped into a hot oven; that is how it feels. It is the first greeting, the first contact with this new world. It is in my nose, in my eyes and in my mouth; I choke on hot air mixed with fuel and dust. The heat penetrates the winter clothes I am wearing and for an instant I feel that I am going to faint. I recover and start walking. In the distance I see a group of people waving but their faces are undistinguishable. As I approach, I recognise the tall man with a shock of red hair: Abraham, my uncle. I have looked at his photo so many times. As I come nearer, still focusing on him, I feel as if I am looking into my grandmother's face, an image long forgotten; the same set jaw and the same blue eyes - one smaller than the other and wandering away out of focus - under orange eyebrows. I hope he does not have the same temperament; I do not have very nice memories of her.

Unlike her, he is smiling, and it is a most welcoming smile, which touches each golden tanned crevice of his face. He wears a light-blue short-sleeved shirt and as I come even nearer, my eyes rest on a patch of sweat on his chest. Besides him stands a dark-skinned lady with a streak of silver that, like a river, crosses her dark hair, which is severely tied back in a bun. She has very white teeth and a very kind face. She is very slim and her head is slightly thrust forward from her round shoulders. I cross the barrier and she engulfs me in her strong wiry arms. She is Mady, Abraham's wife.

Abraham stands still and looks at me. His eyes are red and tears are flowing down his cheeks. 'Esther,' he murmurs. 'Esther, my sister... I am looking at you, Myra, and can't believe it. It is like looking at my dearest sister.'

'Abraham!' Mady turns and looks at him with anxious eyes. 'Please don't make yourself ill! Please, please go and sit down somewhere and take a deep breath. Have you brought your tablets with you? He had heart problems not long ago,' she says, turning to me.

'I am perfectly all right, my dear,' he replies. 'No need to make a fuss,' he continues and gives me a tight hug. Mady lights a cigarette. I notice that her hand is shaking.

After that I embrace my other relatives present, their faces long faded from my childhood memory. It is a very moving moment. The only ones I do not recall are Mady and Abraham, although Mady says that they saw me before departing for Palestine in 1941. I was too young to remember. They left for Palestine on a ship a few months before the *Struma* disaster: the ship that sank in the Black Sea in 1942 after the Turkish authorities towed her out of the port of Limassol, in Cyprus, and set her adrift. *Struma* was torpedoed by a Soviet submarine. On that earlier voyage in 1941which Mady and Abraham took, most people on board were detained on the island of Cyprus; 800 Jews from Romania were on board. It is not known how many people died or survived the eight months of imprisonment in Cyprus. They had to wait for the British Authorities in Palestine to allow them free passage.

We leave the airport in a taxi large enough to take all of us. I am told it is called a *sherout*, meaning a service taxi. I sit between Abraham and Mady, who holds my hand tight and hugs me from time to time. It is very, very hot.

4
THE FAMILY

'Welcome to our country!' Abraham says with pride. His voice is shaky; his emotion is almost palpable. The modern road takes us through dry dusty land, the hot sky barely visible through the layers of sand dancing in the wind. Some blocks of flats of modern design, neglected in appearance, can be seen in the distance. Washing is hanging on long lines over balconies and roof terraces, and blinds are drawn in an effort to keep out the heat of the sun.

'They are old flats where new immigrants are being housed till a more suitable place is found for them. Those buildings are more than 20 years old!'

Is that old? I am thinking, but I say nothing. An idle thought crosses my mind: what is the point of putting the laundry out only for it to turn grey with dust? Even the odd palm tree I notice here and there as the only vegetation is grey with sand.

'What are those square boxes on the roofs?' I ask, as I notice metal cubes, perhaps chimneys, on every building, big or small.

'They are solar water tanks,' they answer in a chorus. 'It was one of our first inventions,' Abraham adds with pride in his voice. 'They are called *doud shemesh*,' and with this, my first Hebrew lesson has begun.

All the way to Hollon, the road, beautifully smooth and straight, cuts through mountains of golden sand. There is no green in the landscape, and to my 'Continental' eyes everything looks parched and almost deserted. Army trucks overtake us or go past the other way on the wide road, raising clouds of sand in their wake. I notice that our driver uses the wipers dry to clear the sand off the windows.

'Wait and see,' Abraham says, catching my bewildered look, 'wait and see how we've changed the landscape, how we have built towns on sand.' Mady nods in agreement. The others say nothing.

Uncle Jean, who is sitting next to the driver, cracks a joke: 'Good country to dry laundry!' We pass by the outer margins of Tel Aviv; rows after rows of blocks of flats, some older, some newer and more under construction. Lots of young people in army uniform, carrying arms and military bags, stand by the roadside, with their thumbs up, requesting and hoping to hitch a lift. The name they use is *tremp*. Lots of private cars are stopping and the soldiers pile inside. I am surprised. I am used to seeing soldiers in grey or khaki army trucks covered with thick canvas, not like those giggling and joking conscripts by the roadside. People have the courage to stop their cars and take on these armed men? Incredible! We turn left without stopping, towards Hollon. There is no room in our taxi for more passengers.

The two towns are separated by a large empty field. The air is hot in the *sherout,* as the air conditioning is unable to cope. Sweat is running down the men's shirts and the women use paper fans. I feel sleepy and make an effort to stay awake. Like everywhere, wherever there is empty, unoccupied and uncultivated land, rubbish, broken furniture, rusty car parts and mattresses find their place. The air is full of rotten food smell.

Houses appear in clusters of a few concrete blocks of flats, arranged around a small square and shops. Then, more sand. Even half-asleep as I am, I cannot stop wondering what sort of house they have. Back home I had visions of a large villa with terraces and orange trees in bloom, like my in-laws and Dan had described when they were reminiscing about Palestine.

We stop at one of those clusters of two-storey buildings, which is raised from the ground and set on concrete stilts. Somebody once must have tried to plant a garden but all is withered now. There are four maisonettes in their building. An outside staircase joins the ground floor maisonette with the upper floor and my uncle's is the ground floor one. Later I would find out that the doors are always open, as neighbours rush in and out of apartments unannounced, without knocking, just to greet each other, see what they are cooking or sewing, or simply for a chat and the latest gossip.

Mady opens the entrance door and I see a large space, all white. It is a very large lounge furnished with simple white furniture: a settee, and a table and chairs of aluminium and Formica of no particular style. The ceiling is white, with a nice wrought-iron ceiling lamp and a revolving fan. The floor, made of mosaic-like large tiles of polished concrete, is also grey-white There are no carpets and no curtains - only roller blinds made out of some plastic material, which is also white. The only dash of colour is a potted ficus plant. Its luscious large green and orange leaves create a focus point. Inside the pot, the soil is dry sand. I think of our yard back home, with the mighty walnut tree surrounded by green grass where the children play. Mady catches my eye and says, 'This is my own little garden.' She is pointing to a stand where a pot with a spider plant and another with dark, almost purple, leaves - which we call back home 'the Wandering Jew'- stand side by side.

It is not at all what I had thought it would be; however, a homely, hopeful, free feeling is somehow generated by this space. I am shown to my room. There is a bed and a built-in wardrobe with thin wooden doors, made from the same material as the blinds. Again, no carpets or curtains. All is simple and functional. I am so glad that I can finally change into a light dress.

Mady gets busy in the kitchen, which is also white Formica. There is a cooker and the largest fridge-freezer I have ever seen. A water tank that gets hot water from the roof tank occupies a large part of the room.

The family fills the lounge: four pairs of uncles and their wives. They all talk at once, asking me about Romania, the people they knew and the streets where they had lived. I do not have the answers. I am too tired to think. Mady moves fast, filling glasses with a diluted grapefruit juice and ice that they call *mitz.* Another word added to my vocabulary. Then she brings plates of pretzels, nuts and olives. The talking continues. I find it funny that they speak Romanian but here and there use nouns in Hebrew. I want to know if it was difficult to learn the new language. All but Abraham shift in their seats, uneasy. Uncle Isaac starts laughing.

'Who said we've learned Hebrew?' says Uncle Jean. 'We picked up a few words here and there, useful for work or the market. There is a lot of Romanian and Yiddish spoken everywhere. Even the Arabs who sell vegetables in Nazareth and Bethlehem have learned Romanian; it's good for business.'

Abraham cuts in, 'There are at least 20 languages spoken in this country. The youngsters mostly learn Hebrew in the army, and then they teach their parents. You are going to be OK. You can't get lost in

Israel; there'll always be someone who understands and can speak to you.'

'This is a country of intellectual, professional people who cannot read or write: illiterates,' Annie, Uncle Leon's wife, chips in, rearranging her erect posture.

Abraham is quiet, unlike his older brother Jean. He speaks, when he does at all, in a quiet voice and he tends to add a joke. I am warming to him. Mady is also full of kindness. She appears to be genuinely happy to see me.

'How is my sister?' Abraham asks. 'Is she happy, healthy?' They have not spoken for many years. 'Such a shame she cut herself off from all of us. Grandfather died with her name on his lips.'

It is true: she did not want to know. I was the one who kept the communication channels open. I reply that she is well, working; she has been the breadwinner since my father lost his job and came out of prison weak and unwell.

'You know, when you appeared at the airport, I had this vision: Esther - not you - was walking towards me. I am sorry that Mady started fussing because last year I had a heart attack.' No wonder then that Mady was so tense.

'How did it happen?' I ask and feel this is a useless, intrusive question.

'Later,' Mady tells me. 'He went through such a lot; I am thankful that he is better,' she says and she hands me a tray full of glasses to carry through to the guests.

'She's already found a job for you, and you've only just arrived. Cruel woman, my wife,' Abraham says with a laugh.

'How are they, my dear cousins?' I turn and ask Uncle Leon.

'Vivy is studying to be a nurse,' Leon says and he looks at Annie, as if for approval. She looks away, tightening her jaw. I smell trouble, a sort of tension.

'How lovely! And Gaby?' I ask.

Tears appear in Leon's eyes. 'She is OK, 'he says. The room falls silent. Obviously, I have asked the wrong question. I promise myself to find out later.

'I am so glad you've arrived, Myra,' Annie adds, breaking the uneasy silence. 'It would be nice to have more educated company, some intellectual talk.' All the others seem to rearrange themselves in their seats.

'My wife suffers from the lack of culture here,' Leon steps in, as if to justify Annie's statement. 'She reads in German; one cannot find Romanian language books here.'

'I brought a few books with me,' I say. 'I would be glad to lend them to her after I've read them myself.'

Leon looks pleased and squeezes Annie's hand.

Annie is tall and one could describe her as majestic; she fills the room with her presence. She is well-groomed and has slightly protruding eyes under well-pencilled-in, designer non-existent eyebrows. Her hair, beautifully set, is like a silver mane framing her face; a handsome, fearsome face. It's very different from that of Aunt Sophie, Leon's first wife and the mother of my cousins. I remember her beauty, her gentleness and her timid smile.

All the time she spent with us, Annie sat erect on the edge of her seat, quite obviously uneasy in the company of her husband's family. But that could be my imagination, trying to read too much into every move, every gesture. Annie wears a well-tailored grey skirt and a white silk blouse. A silver chain adorns her neck – everything matches her silver hair.

The uneasy silence is broken by Abraham, who intervenes with a joke, an anecdote about Israel. The first German immigrants – all or most of them highly educated people – who arrived in the aftermath of the war expected to find well-appointed houses and university places for them to teach. Once they became acquainted with the reality, they rolled up their sleeves and set to work to build the country. It was said that they formed tidy chains and, addressing each other with perfect manners, they would pass the bricks from one to the other, saying, '*Bitte, Her Doktor*' and '*Danke, Her Doktor*' in the most formal manner.

That makes everyone smile and the festive atmosphere is restored. Annie says nothing; she adjusts her posture and crosses her long well-shaped legs. Obviously, she does not share their sense of humour. Leon looks uneasy. It seems to me that one moment he is joining in the light conversation and banter, but the next he is looking anxiously at his wife, as if to ascertain her reaction. That's what he did earlier when he spoke about Gaby and said that she was OK. It was the moment when my Aunt Golda touched my arm discreetly and I understood that I had strayed into a difficult topic.

The atmosphere is turning oppressive again and Uncle Isaac starts singing an old Romanian song full of cheerful words and innuendos, and the mood lightens once again. Finally, the visitors get up to leave, each taking turns for hugs and warm kisses, and they invite me to come and spend time with them. Annie and Leon live in Jerusalem and they invite me to spend a week with them. They are very proud of their newly acquired apartment. They point out repeatedly how, in spite of difficulties not of their own making, they have achieved a home and a good living. Leon, the large, gentle giant that I always knew, seems to be very emotional. He laughs and cries almost simultaneously. I have not seen him since he was liberated from prison and emigrated with this new wife and his two teenage daughters. He speaks of the time he spent in the salt mines in Romania, like most upper- and middle-class people who were incarcerated by the Communist regime, as the best life experience he could ever have had. Bravado? I can't help wondering.

Leon and Annie are the first to leave. I do not know Annie, but the whole afternoon I have had the feeling that she was not at ease and that she could not wait for the moment when she could get away.

As soon as they are gone, everyone starts speaking at once, all reserve gone. Uncle Jean is the first, his Adam's apple turning crimson: 'Who do they think they are? All those airs and graces! Have you noticed how Leon sips the words from that woman's lips?'

It brought back memories of Uncle Jean from when I was a child: his show-off attitude, always very opinionated. It appears that he has found his match in his second wife, Fanny. She loses no time in joining her husband's tirade. 'This woman, the way she treated the children... unspeakable! They put poor Gaby in the mental hospital and now that she is better and due to come home, this woman refuses to take her in. And he does not say a word!'

'What happened to Gaby?' I ask with a tremor in my voice. I have fond memories of my cousin; the serious, scholarly, studious girl - only a few years younger than me - who, at some time in her life, was alone to fend for herself and take care of her younger sister. Leon, her father, was serving time in a Romanian prison; the mother abandoned them as well and the stepmother would not have them. My father and I used to bring them food parcels once a month and pay a neighbour to look after them when she could.

'We don't really know what happened to Gaby. They would not talk about her.'

Isaac and Golda are next to leave. They also ask me to come and stay with them. I know them better, as I used to go to their apartment in Bucharest with my mother and sister during our annual visits to them. They also live in central Tel Aviv and I think I will ask Isaac's help in my quest to find George's people. I will also find out more about what is going on.

5
AMNON

The day I meet my cousin Amnon, he barely acknowledges me. Mady comes forward and gives him a hug. Her anxious eyes search his intently, expecting some answers. He is young, although his stocky build and a thick moustache make it hard to ascertain his age. 'This is Myra!' Mady says. I move forward to embrace him but he turns to his mother and says, 'I want a bath.' For a fraction of a second, I stay put with my outstretched arms in the air.

'Do you want something to eat, darling?' Mady asks her son.

He replies in Hebrew and shakes his head. Then he leaves the room without another word. I can hear the shower running, and a trickle of water and suds appear in the living room. Mady hastens to fetch the mop, shaking her head. I say nothing.

Then she tells me, speaking quietly, that he is upset because, after spending a week with the army for assessment, he has been rejected at the medical examination. No conscription for him. He also failed his driving test. 'He wanted so much to join the army and be like all his friends!' Mady is in tears. 'What will his father say? I hope Abraham won't be hard on him. He sometimes expects too much.' She turns to me. 'Don't worry about Amnon; he will get over it. In any case, he is going to appeal.'

Appeal? We were so happy when Dan was rejected from military service on the grounds that he was too thin, below standard weight. That meant that he could continue to work - he was the only breadwinner at the time - and also complete his studies at night classes.

And here I am, listening to this mother saying that she and the family are upset because her son can't join the war and the killings. Everything is upside-down.

She follows the boy and starts fussing round him, anxious and sad, and I have the feeling that she wants to fold her strong arms round him and shield him from all the knocks that life may have in store for him. That is the way I feel about Nicky. I am thinking that perhaps that is why I am here.

I feel that my presence is not wanted and decide to go out for a walk, although the sun is fierce at midday. I'll walk as far as the cluster of prefabs about half a mile away, where I was told that Anna – my old landlady from the time of my medical training – is living with her husband Yasha. I arrive, hot and sweaty, after walking for a good mile. And there they are: Anna looking the same, as if the years have not touched her. There is a little patch of land at the front, where the couple sit on two rusty chairs in the shade provided by an old canopy. Their house is a prefab one-bedroom bungalow. The patch of green is littered with a collection of dustbins, chairs, brooms, rags and an improvised outdoor shower - such a contrast to their apartment in Udrican! They look serene and unchanged. To my surprise, in the neighbouring prefab, almost the same as their own, live Rosa - Anna's sister - and her husband. They tell me that they have refused the offer of re-housing in a concrete-built block of flats. They are happy where they are. They do not have to pay rent or maintenance, which they could not afford, and the neighbours are friendly. They are like a big family. I am thinking of the elegant apartment I shared with them in central Bucharest, with the walls covered in stucco painted light cream, and Yasha throwing his weight about as the building's administrator. But they had to take me as a lodger because they could not afford the rent and charges. It looks to me that although they had come all this way, they did not find a bonanza.

Anna asks me how I am getting on with Abraham and Mady. I reply that I thought I was getting on well; I really liked them. And I met Amnon.

'You will soon meet Emmanuel, their pride and joy,' says Anna. Then she starts talking about Amnon. 'Abraham is so tough on the poor boy, while your grandmother - may she rest in peace - and Mady spoiled him. Poor Mady had a lot to cope with. Did they not write to you about his accident?'

'No, they only wrote about Emmanuel, how he became a naval officer, and sent us a picture of his wedding. You know how it is with our family: illnesses and accidents are considered personal failures, so we don't talk about them.'

'Of course they would not talk about poor Amnon, but they would boast about Emmanuel. He was sent to France and graduated there, and he married a girl from a rich family. Her father, one of the founders of the State, was an architect and a strong influence on the development of the new towns. Abraham could only be proud of this son. But the other was left in the shadows.' After a while Anna said: 'Your grandma used to say that he was tolerated rather than loved.'

'So tell me about Amnon!'

'Amnon fell off a tall palm tree. He must have been about seven, long before we arrived. Your grandma used to visit us and tell us what a lively boy he was. She told us how on that dreadful day the other kids were screaming but Amnon lay still on the ground. After that fall, he spent months and months in Hadassah hospital in Jerusalem. When he came home, he had rages and temper tantrums, rolling wildly and thrashing on the floor. She told us, crying, how she and Mady tried to restrict and pacify him, and shield him from Abraham when he came home from work. Abraham does not have much patience with the boy.'

On my return, I find Amnon sitting alone and eating a late dinner, with Mady standing by and serving him. He is slightly more communicative and I am more prepared to make allowances for him, after my conversation with Anna.

'How is Bucharest?' he asks in heavily accented Romanian. 'Have you got pavements like we have and buildings like we have?'

I think of the elegant pavements at home, made of slabs of granite set in a pattern, and I am tempted to reply, 'Well, not like these.' However, I just nod and I hope that the irony does not show in my face.

'Did you come to stay?' he asks next.

'For the present I am visiting and it is lovely to know you,' I reply, slightly offended by his directness.

He keeps his sulky teenager's expression and wipes his thick moustache with the serviette. While he is eating, I notice that he has a tremor in his left arm. He stands up and tells his mother that he is going somewhere. I notice that he walks with a slight limp.

'Where to?' she asked.

'Out' is the reply.

6
INSIGHT

Two months fly by; two long months full of new discoveries, new sensations, new ideas and new insights into a world previously unknown to me. Two months of longing and contradictory emotions, of incessant searching for a decision which is possibly going to change the rest of my life.

The Six-Day War is over. Most men have come home from the front and returned to their previous occupations. People have started to travel again and to explore the newly attached territories, pretending that nothing of importance has happened. But the anxiety remains in the hearts and minds, whether it is acknowledged or not. Every hour, on the hour, everyone I meet listens to the news bulletin, the *hadashot*. Everyone stops working or whatever else they are doing in order to listen, holding their breaths, to the news from the front: the army bulletins, new exchange of fire, counting the dead and assessing the damage. Most of all, people want to make sure that the names of their nearest and dearest are not on the list of casualties. The fact that the other side lost lives as well is never mentioned. Immediately after the news, the radio breaks into song and in the sound of music people return to their daily chores. The sound of gaiety lasts another hour, till the next bulletin.

Mady and Abraham return to their daily routine: Abraham leaves first, after breakfast, and goes to open the shop. Their small business in the shopping centre sells household goods and kitchen utensils. Mady stays behind at home to tidy up, do the washing, tidy the clothes scattered about - mostly by the youngest son, Amnon, who is still living at home - and prepare lunch. Not long after my arrival, I take over these chores and Mady is most grateful. She is a lovely woman: quick, efficient, uncomplaining, and she never speaks ill of anyone. After lunch Mady goes to the shop to take over from Abraham, who returns home for lunch and a rest, as the doctor advised. Once a week they go to their friends, or their friends come to them, to play rummy and to laugh and chat. My stay gives me a good insight into their life. They are not rich but they have all that is necessary for everyday living. They rarely eat out and never go to the cinema or the theatre, and I do not see them reading anything other than the daily newspaper. There are no books in the house.

During the hours we spend together, Mady tells me a bit about their life since they arrived in Palestine in 1941. They had been kept in Cyprus for about six months before they obtained permission to enter Palestine. Once they left the ship in the harbour of Haifa, men and women were separated and put in different camps. They used to meet for a chat in the evening by the fence. The British Crown did not allow free movement of the new immigrants in Palestine. There was opposition from the native Palestinians. After the first year, the colonial power relented, as news of the World War atrocities from Germany and Poland permeated. The couple were very poor and Abraham found work on an Arab's farm. That year Mady became pregnant with their first child, and Emmanuel was born the following year. Around that time, Abraham joined the Haganah. He felt that freedom and independence would not happen unless the people fought for it. After 1948 and the independence, they were housed in Hollon. They struggled but by 1947-48 money from Romania started to arrive. It was from Leon, who was sending his wealth in preparation for his own exit from Romania. In 1949 Abraham's elderly parents, Moshe and Risl - my grandparents - arrived and there was a need for larger accommodation. Abraham was meant to keep Leon's hard currency for when he arrived, but he now had elderly parents and his own children to support. He used part of the money to buy a small shop. This way he would ensure a steady source of income. The rest he invested on Leon's behalf in some emerging business. He told himself that Leon would not object - after all, it was for the benefit of their parents. Leon would be pleased that he had found a secure place and made the money grow. However, his investments proved to be a failure and he lost most of Leon's money. When Leon finally arrived, together with his second wife and his two daughters, their expectations met with disappointment. Leon never forgave his brother for ruining him. Abraham was trying to pay back his debt but the rift was so wide that it appeared no bridge could be built over it.

I was beginning to understand the tensions, the bad feelings, within the family. Oh God, what had I stepped into? I hoped I was not going to be involved in any of this. I vaguely understood why Leon got a job at a bank and lived modestly on a salary, and why Abraham felt it was not his fault that he lost all that money. I was thinking that we never had such problems, because we never had any money. Every fortnight we eagerly awaited our salaries. By the time the money arrived, we were already in debt. Firstly, we had to pay back what we had borrowed during the previous week; then we gave our parents enough for the weekly shopping and housekeeping, and finally, we kept a little pocket money for ourselves. If there was a little extra, we sent it to my parents who were also struggling. My sister - and also Dan's younger sister - needed help with her education. The cake, as they say, was being cut in very thin slices.

7
REFLECTIONS

What happened to me during those two months is so packed with facts and thoughts that it's almost too difficult to relate and even more difficult to explain.

I felt like a child again. With child's eyes full of wonder, I was looking at this world. It was a new world, almost in its infancy, built on sand and heat - a tough world with wars and enemies who tried to nip it in the bud. Many of those enemies were displaced and refused - and still continue to refuse - to recognise its existence. But it continued to exist and to grow with hope, belief and determination. Jews who had been known in Europe as involved with commerce, money and trade were becoming farmers, gardeners, fishermen, sailors and factory workers. As one comic strip caption stated, 'Even the street sweepers and dustmen are Jewish.' I was more familiar with my folks being doctors, lawyers, teachers, musicians and writers. The *moshavs* - villages - were flourishing; the kibbutz communities were adapting the cultivation of plants to dry environment conditions. They were the first to discover that if they surrounded cultivated land with tall fern trees and cypresses, the crops would be protected from the hot destructive winds and would invite the clouds to unload their rain. They used solar power, albeit primitively and unsightly, to warm water so that one could take a shower or a bath anytime.

Jews who had been excluded from various European armies, who were perceived as shy of wars and battles, became warriors - ready to defend their new country and ready to die for it. Look at my cousin Amnon and all his friends!

We, the ones left behind in Europe, would not dream of joining the army and our young men - Jews and non-Jews - did everything in their power to avoid conscription. Here were girl-soldiers, girl-police and they looked so happy!

I was a child again. All decisions were taken away from me. I did not have to worry about where the next meal was coming from or what new clothes I could afford; I did not have to decide who I would visit or see. This was all decided for me and I was happy to fit in, trying not to cause offence. I spent a few weeks with a couple of relatives - Uncle Isaac and Aunt Golda - first in their luxurious apartment in Tel Aviv and then on their annual holiday to Safed where we visited the Sea of Galilee. I imagined myself walking the walk of the prophets from Cana to Galilee. It was here, it is said, that Jesus preached. It was here, at the lowest freshwater lake in the world, that he found his followers among the fishermen: Simon, his brother Andrew, and the other brothers John and James. They earned their livelihood from the pure water of Kineret that later, in the first century, was named the Tiberias Sea. It was on this fertile land, the story goes, that Jesus had preached the famous Sermon on the Mount and performed his miracles. That is what I remembered from lessons taught to my classmates by Father Ivan long, long ago when a seven-year-old me, frustrated and humiliated for being left outside, listened through the shut classroom door.

And here, in the first century of modern times, the Jews, forbidden to enter Jerusalem after rebelling against the Romans, established their centre and wrote the Jerusalem Talmud.

I also stayed with Leon and Annie and visited Jerusalem, the golden city, with its dome and churches, and the tower of David. I walked the Via Dolorosa and saw the ancient Coptic Church of the Nativity. There are two churches, one next to the other, each claiming the privilege of guarding over Jesus's tomb.

Then Abraham took a vacation. He left the shop in Mady's care and took me on a bus tour around the country, from Jerusalem to the Dead Sea and from there to the Red Sea, through small towns - dots of dusty green on a sea of miles and miles of arid desert land. I bathed in the warm, shallow springs of Engedi and felt like Eve among the fertile luscious gardens, ready to entice Adam. The bus took us to the ancient city of King Avdalga. I sat on his throne and pretended I was his queen. Massada, the ruined fortress, and the Herodotus palaces had been excavated in the previous few years. It was the place where the rebel Jews who fled Jerusalem were defeated by the Romans in 66 C.E. The defeated rebels committed mass suicide rather than surrender. The thought was appealing. Yes, suicide. If I could not see my child again, that is what I would do. I only hoped I would be so brave.

On and on the bus progressed, through heat and dust, past Beersheba, the Negev capital, and the new towns of Dimona and Arad down to the Dead Sea. I walked on water and imagined how Jesus is said to have done it. On we travelled, through the desert. The awe-inspiring, dream-like gigantic, golden red columns of Solomon's temple appeared, majestically dominating the horizon. We were told that nobody knew whether they were man-made or a natural rock formation. When the sun descended over the horizon, another giant golden rock, like a giant mushroom, turned blood-red, as if on fire. Yes, I understood how legends were created, how people felt so small and why they bowed to the grandeur and eternity of creation.

At the Red Sea in Eilat we spent the night in a modest hotel. The next day we took a boat and saw a myriad of coloured fish through the boat's glass bottom. Across the sea stood the gleaming white ancient Akaba town, where people were living so near that you could see them, almost touch them, and yet were millions of years apart in their beliefs and their hatred.

On my return, I went to visit Haifa and fell in love with the garden of the Bahais, their temple and their art, which spread from the top of Mount Carmel all the way down to the sea. It was so peaceful, shady and quiet; a place to think and stare. I walked down the hundred steps, each one bordered by silver tulips which trembled in the breeze. I sat in the shade of exotic trees and meditated while I looked down at the distant shimmering sea. What made me so unhappy back home? Unhappy enough to consider dismantling my whole past, all I had previously known and lived with?

Where I come from, houses are solid, built with stones and bricks. Church steeples, minarets and the domes of synagogues are defining points of what we are. It is true that those symbols are lying almost deserted and attendance is not encouraged, but they are there, giving solidity to our roots. Each day when we pass them by, we are reminded of our history, our suffering and our moments of joy.

Back home we have concert halls and theatres, libraries and museums. All right, they are under strict censorship and many books are no longer present in libraries; theatre plays are selected by the powerful, who are afraid of their subversive content, but there are still the classics to enjoy and it is possible even then to read the message between the lines.

Here there are mountains of empty rocks, thirsty for water.

Back home we have mountains which soar to the sky, covered in miles of forests of oak trees and fir trees, meadows covered in flowers and rivers which flow down, searching the sea.

We have the choice to take two weeks' annual paid leave and go to the mountains or to the sea. We cannot afford hotels or to buy food in resort shops, so we take provisions with us from home and sleep in shacks, rent a room from the locals or stay with family. If we spend more than three days away from home, we have to register with the police. It is this oppressive control that is unbearable. *Freedom*. Freedom is what we crave.

Here people live in new blocks of flats with little care for aesthetics, but they have a place of their own. They don't have to share kitchens and bathrooms with strangers; they don't have eight cubic metres of air to breathe in. They can breathe freely. How many metres of cubic air does a caged bird need? The basic needs of a civilised person are fulfilled here: cold and hot water, a choice of food on the table, and the right to choose a place of work according to their and their family's needs. Here one is not arrested for wearing his hair long or short, or if one sports a beard or dresses a little out of the ordinary. Here people can do whatever they like with their money; if they have any to spare, they can keep it at home or in the banks, or travel wherever and whenever they want. They are not frightened to say out loud what they think; nobody is listening in and reporting their neighbour, and the police officers are friendly and concerned with the protection of the neighbourhood rather than punishing or abusing its inhabitants. Of course, there are restrictions here as well, but they do not extend to the basic needs of human beings. I would like to live in this free world and bring up my child in an environment where she will have a choice and be master of her destiny.

Back home we cannot speak freely; we cannot complain. Here, in this new world, all seem to shout out loud, without constraint, whatever words or ideas pass through their mind. The children are raised without fear and encouraged to have an opinion. Manners and conventions are thrown to the wind, discarded as a relic of the past. I wish my Nicky were here; she would fit in beautifully.

Besides, I made a promise and I need to prove to myself that I can do it. And I have to prove to my family that I am the one who can help them to fulfil their dream.

In Tel Aviv I stay with Uncle Isaac again for a fortnight. My visa will expire at the end of November and time is running out. We locate one of the members of the group in George's photograph.

The other one we identified is an important leader and his address can't be easily obtained. The chances of gaining entrance directly to the Knesset, the parliament in Jerusalem, are minimal. My uncle telephones and speaks in Hebrew to the first person on the list, whose address is the nearest to our location - a Mr Cohen - but he promptly refuses to have anything to do with this. He does not even listen to the whole story but, at my uncle's insistence, takes down the name, although he assures my uncle that he has no knowledge whatsoever of George.

Well, that is that. My uncle never mentions the matter again, presumably so as not to hurt my feelings or embarrass me. I think that the decision has been made for me; once my holiday visa expires, I will return home. I failed my mission and I feel quite relieved. Two days later the telephone rings and Uncle Isaac answers it. When he puts the phone back on the stand, he looks quite stunned. 'It was a person calling on behalf of that Mr Cohen. He asked to see the photos and confirm a contact number. How did they get my number? I did not leave a name or a number!'

My heart gives a jolt, and I cannot speak. All I can think is: *Here I go again; everything is turning around once again*.

My aunt looks happy. 'Does that mean Myra can stay?'

'Golda don't jump the gun! Nothing is clear to me; this man did not even leave a name.' Isaac looks cross, as he usually does when speaking to his wife. I feel so sorry for her, being put down like that.

'I do not want to part with the photos,' I say, once I recover my voice.

'That's no problem. There is a good photographer near us; we'll make copies.'

He looks preoccupied and says, 'I am going to speak to Abraham first and then maybe with your cousin Karol. He works for the Sochnut, the immigration organisation. Mind you, he is such a klutz; he may not have any answers.'

Isaac picks up the phone again and has long conversations with my other uncles while I sit next to Aunt Golda, holding her hand. I am thinking that again matters have been taken out of my hands and wondering if these things can be discussed on the telephone: is it safe? Apparently, yes. Freedom!

We have copies made and send them by post to Mr Cohen's address. Not long after, I am walking down the long Ben Yehuda Street with my uncle to a basement flat located at the end of town, in Jaffo. We find a modest flat and a wheezy old man: Mr Cohen is severely afflicted by asthma. He is a skinny elderly man, probably George's age, with a face that reminds me of a mouse; his chest heaves with his laboured breathing. The meeting is short. He speaks in Hebrew and Uncle Isaac translates. He wants to know how George is, although only the day before he said that he had never met him. I am not going to argue and ask why he was in the photograph, next to George. He turns towards me and, speaking in English, he suggests that I should extend my stay.

8
SHOULD I STAY OR SHOULD I GO?

Should I stay or go back? If I return, what am I to expect? Awake night after night with stomach pains, the ulcer that I acquired during my spell in the country raises its head every time I am exhausted or worried. Should I go back and join my colleagues in courting even the hospital porter and driver, because they are known to be distantly related to the powerful first lady, Elena Ceausescu, who was born to a family from a village nearby? The world would have been a happier place without her but there it was; we needed this connection to have even a hope of getting what we wanted. Each of us hoped that the driver would put in a good word for us and achieve what our exams could not: a job in Bucharest, where our families were.

And supposing I achieve that, what next? A family doctor in an industrial town like Bucharest is expected to visit factories and offices every month to examine unsuspecting women - who do not have the right to refuse such intrusive examination - and report any sign of pregnancy or recent abortions. That is just because the Government has ordered more children and has forbidden contraception. Some said that, under Ceausescou's orders, the factories producing condoms were instructed to produce faulty goods with small perforations, in order to fulfil the leader's dream of increasing the Romanian population. Perhaps this was a joke, but what was for sure was that doctors, nurses and midwives were arrested if they were caught performing illegal abortions, and many women who had the procedure ended up dead or in prison. Do I want to be part of this? Is that what I want?

The truth, or part of it, is that I am not happy within myself. Ever since the birth of my daughter I have had moments when I found myself ugly and dull. My intelligence has suffered a downward spiral with every entrance examination failure. In each attempt I have found myself one or two points below the minimum mark required to be offered a place in the capital. Even when I achieved top marks for the professional part, the social note brought down the average. Each time I did less well, even in the professional part. Finally, I got a place for training in a specialty: nutrition and public health, for a post at Gaesti Hospital after I completed my training. A provincial hospital, 60 kilometres from Bucharest, on the main Bucharest–Pitesti train line. I had to take it. I could not - I would not - return to Seaca, where I had spent the first three years of my professional life. One year of training at the faculty in Bucharest made me realise that although the course was interesting, it was not what I wanted. But I could be near Nicky, see her grow a little more each day. To be a family doctor or a specialist in Internal Medicine, look after the sick and improve their health – that was what I wanted. But that had to be postponed. My morale was low and my health poor. But depression was not to be mentioned in my family. 'Grin and bear it; it will pass,' was our motto. After the year of training, the commuting to Gaesti Hospital started. It was not far, only 40 miles from Bucharest, but there were only two trains a day, and the journey took two hours on the faster train and three on the slow one. The first train was at 7 o'clock so each morning I got up before daylight at 4 a.m. George got up first and went to the kitchen to make coffee and some sandwiches for all of us, the ones who went to work. He didn't have to sign in, nor did he have to meet the formidable hospital secretary whose job was to report to the Director any late arrivals. I had to leave before daybreak if I was to be at the hospital for 9 o'clock. If the train was late, the hospital secretary, who was the wife of the Director, would glare at me and I used to shrink under her gaze. I was so tired! But I got through the day. Then it was a fight against time to finish what I had to do so as not to miss the 6 o'clock train. It was crowded, but I would have a seat held by my other colleagues from further up the line. We all squeezed into the one compartment. A large medical bag was placed in the space between facing seats and we played canasta; others were knitting or embroidering. I made a pullover for Dan with the wool I had unravelled from a comforter imported from China which I had found by chance in a shop. I was so happy to have found it! I had bought two and had enough wool to make Nicky a dress. If I turned my eyes discreetly to the left, I could see Rocco caressing Petra's back and Paul, the radiologist, exchanging furtive kisses with the microbiologist. On my right, Eugene was making passes at Valerie. I was pleased to sit next to Marius and let our hands touch from time to time. Each one of us had a husband or a wife and children at home. The commuter crowd was like a cesspit of lost souls lacking in moral sense and self-respect. I wanted out; I wanted to escape. It was not only my husband and his parents and sisters who wanted out – it was me too! I kept telling myself that my daughter did not need me, that she was being brought up by her grandma, and at times she did not even come near me.

If we get out perhaps even my husband will change, become more responsible. I blame him for not making any effort to make our life easier, not being master in his own house and living under his father's rule just because it is convenient. I know I am being bitter and unfair and looking for someone to blame.

Yes, he is right and this man, Cohen, is right too: the only hope is for me to stay. So I stay. Once again, the decision is taken out of my hands. In the words of Claudia Gould: *We are leaves driven before the wind*

9
BUONGIORNO ITALY

It is a little late to ask myself again, what am I doing here? How did I end up in such a situation? Too late. I am on a flight to Italy, courtesy of the Israeli Government. No one knows where I am, except my Israeli uncles and aunts, who knew where I was going but have no details. I've promised to inform them of my whereabouts as soon as I know myself.

I am sitting on my old cardboard suitcase, the one that accompanied me from Bucharest on my journey to Tel Aviv and now to Rome. I arrived at Fiumicino Airport earlier this December morning at 11 o'clock. I came prepared for winter but it is warm in the airport. I am waiting on the tarmac to collect my suitcase and carry it into the terminal, thinking how uncivilised this is: even in Romania or Tel Aviv you would collect the luggage in the hall. In the concourse nobody is waiting for me, so I wait. It is almost past 1 o'clock and I am still waiting. Nobody calls my name; nobody is here to look for me. I remove the warm tweed coat that Uncle Isaac made for me. In my pocket I have a $20 bill, a present from Uncle Abraham, which I keep touching in case I lose it. But it is of no use to me at this moment. I don't know where to change it into Italian liras and the crowd is so dense that I can't see anything advertised, nor do I know how to use a public phone here. I don't know the country's code or how to operate it. I am thirsty and, the question of money aside, I do not dare to leave the spot where I have been told to wait in case I miss the person sent to meet me.

Again and again I try to make sense of the recent events. All I ever wanted was to have a quiet life, with my husband and daughter in my own place, to practice the profession I love and respect with all its up-and-down moments, and to give Nicky a stable home, a good education and a future. Perhaps I want too much. Perhaps I want what other people have or appear to have: a say in the running of their own lives, the freedom of choice. Perhaps it is not meant to be.

Still, here I am, as advised by the officials from Jerusalem a couple of weeks ago: leave Israel and, at their expense, take a short trip to Rome and then return to Israel as a new immigrant. Only then can they intervene, via the Red Cross, and allow me to bring my husband and daughter.

By the time I was informed of that decision, it was already too late to return to Romania without suffering serious repercussions. My visa had expired two months earlier. I had overstayed, waiting for an answer. The authorities took their time. The letters from home became increasingly insistent, encouraging me, in veiled terms, to stay on and do everything in my power to get them out of there. I understood their desperate wish. It was a mission, a promise I meant to fulfil.

In the airport around me time moves on and with it my anxiety mounts. Finally, I decide to go to the information desk. I do not speak Italian, or English, but with my Romanian and the Latin I learned at school I ought to make myself understood. The answer is negative; nobody has called but the pretty young woman who is speaking to me from behind the glass wall explains: 'There is a strike on, a general strike in Rome, and nothing is moving. For the last six hours no one has been able to reach the airport, nor can any passengers that have arrived leave. The airport staff, the taxis and even the telephone lines are at a standstill.'

I understand almost every word but I find it hard to reply or ask some more questions. Now I understand why I had to carry my own suitcase from the plane on the tarmac. I also know that I have to stay put and wait. All of a sudden, I hear the rhythmic movement of a crowd marching and I see them walking by, in compact rows, carrying flags and banners. They whistle and shout in rhythm with the march, '*Stupido*! *Stupido*!' I presume that is addressed to the government and not to us innocent bystanders.

After a time I ask the woman behind the glass window, the best I can, if she could tell me how to use the coin telephone and if she could change a $20 bill. She laughs so loud that the double row of chunky amber beads round her long, graceful neck dances with her laughter. She takes from her desk a plastic token and hands it to me. Then she writes down on a piece of paper the country codes for Romania and for Israel. 'Tap the code in, wait for a different tone and then dial the number,' she says.

I thank her, take my coat, my handbag and my suitcase, and walk to the telephone. I am still thirsty but that will have to wait.

'Hello, how are things?' I ask Dan when he picks up the phone.

'Ah, it's you. How come you've remembered to phone?'

'Oh, what do you mean? Do you know where I am? Are you in a bad mood? Has anything happened I should know? Is Nicky all right?'

'Yes, she is fine. No, I don't know where you are! I don't know anything anymore! I don't know what to believe.'

'I am in Italy. That is where I am phoning from. I do not think we should talk for very long, for your sake.'

'We had a visit, not a nice one. Your things were taken.'

'Everything? Did they do you any harm?'

'Not really. I was demoted. The colleagues were very sympathetic. The income has remained the same, only my responsibilities have changed.'

'At least you will have enough to survive. Is Mammy back and working again?'

'No, she could not! When she came back, she found that the woman you appointed to care for Nicky was a walking disaster. Mammy had to take over.'

'Oh dear, what shall I do? Come back?'

'No, don't do that! You would end up in detention… That is all I need!'

'Well, this is making me very miserable. I took this risk to give you the message that they - you know who - sent: you and Nicky should fill in new application forms and start the process all over again. This time it is likely to work.'

After a pause he says, the tone of his voice changed, 'Whoa, this is good news! A new start. Marvellous! I hope all goes well!'

'Then why were you so different at the start? What's up?'

'Nothing. I just thought… I don't know… I believed you had left us all behind.'

'What gave you that idea?'

'There were rumours. You see, my sister Lydia heard something. I did not believe it at first, but then…'

'So what? There are always rumours, but I thought we agreed that whatever was going to be, we would never take any notice of it!'

'Yes, but Lydia and Len took a trip over to where you spend most of your days and conducted an enquiry.'

'Was that with your permission? And you believed it all! Anyway, what right did she have to meddle?'

'I am sorry, so very sorry!'

'Never mind. I have passed you the instructions so do as you think fit. Can I speak to my daughter now?'

After a small pause, I hear my little girl's voice.

'Hello Nicky, this is Mummy... Mummy who loves you very much... and hopes to see you soon.'

10
FINDING MY WAY

Finally, the strike is over and the information desk receives a call. I am to be put in a taxi and dispatched to an address in Rome. Do I care where I am going? Not in the least. I feel faint. After that talk on the telephone, the thought that everything I do is in vain does not leave me; it turns and twists in my tired mind. The distance has increased the gap between me and my family; the hole is bigger and I am about to fall in it.

The taxi drops me at Pensione Donna Maria, not far from the Coliseum, just off Via Cavour. It has an imposing façade in white marble, with the entrance guarded by two lions. I am ushered to my room by two pleasant young Israelis. Exhausted, I climb on to the soft comfortable bed, fully dressed as I am, and close my eyes. When I open them again, the white December morning light filters through the windows. I turn on to my back and look at the ornate ceiling with the magnificent cut-glass lamp with a large fan attached. I lie there, and thoughts about my family and home return.

I picture Dan, feeling miserable and abandoned, and worn down by jealousy. He must feel pretty awful; harassed at work and brainwashed at home, the seeds of negative feelings sown in him. I can almost see him, his skinny arms with prominent veins showing whenever he removes the long-sleeved shirt and loosens the tie that he always wears. His grey trousers are always crumpled but his coat correctly buttoned – top and middle buttons. He wears a waistcoat as well, even in summer. I can hear him coughing, which he often does with a loud throaty sound that echoes. I can see his head bent down low, buried in a newspaper, his untamed hair standing up. He and his father discussing in detail each article they are reading.

He was never possessive or jealous. What happened to him? And why did Lydia go to my hospital to make inquiries? She, the pleasant woman I have known for as long as I have known Dan and always admired for her quiet beauty, her green eyes, her smile and her intelligence. She was my friend and I helped her when she needed me. We were close before she married. She changed once she was persuaded to break up with her beloved friend and made to marry Len, the son of a family friend, instead. Her sweet smile turned bitter. Len proved to be a control freak and her own behaviour altered after her marriage. We spent our pregnancies together and our daughters were born only three weeks apart. I cannot understand what has happened. I cannot be bothered with all this. Now that I have embarked on this adventure I am on my own and there is no way back.

To visit a country and see nothing of it – that must be a unique experience. But that is how I walk around Rome. To think how much I longed to visit this magnificent city! The pictures in old books and reproductions of famous old masters' paintings that I could instantly recall are here to touch and see. And here I am and see nothing.

Although I was given some money and told to enjoy myself, since formalities will take about a week, I prefer to stay in my room or walk along Via Cavour. As for the Coliseum, I promise myself that one day I will visit it with Nicky and Dan. Nicky will be old enough to understand by then, and have a better outlook and knowledge of the world than I do. It will be a proper holiday.

My thoughts drift back to home. Our first holiday with Nicky was by the seaside; Nicky fast asleep surrounded by all my high-heeled shoes. She must have been trying to walk like Mummy, long after our hosts, who were babysitting, had fallen asleep.

The day comes to return to Israel. I visit the consular agency, am given an immigration certificate and then I go for a medical at the Ospedale Israelitico. It smells of carbolic and feels like a medieval hospice, with its thick stone vaults and stone stairs. This time the flight, the Aliyah to the Holy Land, is uneventful. There is no family to greet me on my ascent to the chosen country – just the Immigration Agency. They ask if I have any preference for accommodation and language school, and I reply that I do not. They say that they have vacancies at Dimona.

Dimona is as good as any place. I nod in agreement and say, 'OK.'

Tourist, defector, immigrant - all in the month of December. A drop in the ocean of life.

11
BACK TO SCHOOL - DIMONA, 1969

Sifra walks into the classroom with her usual unsmiling stern face, the face of a matron begrudging the happiness of mortals who happen to be her students. She who must be obeyed! She looks larger than ever, thick around the waist, and she walks like a man. I am sure she must have been a rugby player in a previous life - or perhaps a sumo wrestler. She is a contrast to the luminous classroom, which is freshly painted in creamy white and furnished with comfortable chairs and desks. We are 12 adult pupils who seem to become smaller in her presence.

'*Boker tov*!' she greets us.

'*Boker tov*,' we reply in a chorus, like well-behaved children. Our average age is about 45. I think I am the youngest.

She is a trained teacher, and I find her useful and competent. She has an American sort of directness, a no-nonsense approach. Sifra teaches us Hebrew by Hebrew only. She shows no sympathy or mercy for whoever does not come up to her expectations.

The Romanian couple from up north complain bitterly and so does Lionel from Bucharest. He is not used to taking orders from anyone. Adele, a woman in her fifties with mousy, straight hair, makes more of an effort. The two elderly academics from Poland do not complain but you can see them muttering their discontent between themselves. The professor makes good progress. He has the advantage of knowing the alphabet, probably from his bar mitzvah, but his wife is a little slower. She looks distinguished with her silver-grey chignon and her long legs. She must have been a beauty in her youth.

I do my best and in the short while I have spent here I have made progress. Studying keeps me sane, saves me thinking all the time.

'Today we shall talk about strike!' is Sifra's pronounconcrete. '*Shveetah*! When workers do not work!'

Everyone, me included, looks bewildered.

'You know the word "work"! To work, to do something!' Sifra is showing her impatience. She is getting quite annoyed; she starts moving about and picks up a hammer that she brought in the other day to explain the word "work".

'Work! Don't you lot remember anything? It was only yesterday we learned it: *Avodah*!'

Finally, even Mr Katz from northern Romania manages to smile and understands.

Then Sifra starts again the demonstration in incomprehensible Hebrew words: 'Not work, go home, do nothing!' Not getting any response, Sifra mouths a rude word and starts hammering - that means work. Then, shaking her finger, she crosses her arms and sits down still; that equals not work.

Mr Katz is in tears; his wife is patting his hand for comfort. Lionel is nudging me in the ribs, a question mark in his eyes. I wave him away, trying to concentrate. Sifra continues with her exercise: work, not work. She begins to look quite desperate. Then Adele, in a moment of clarity, shouts out: 'Aha, strike, *greve, shvitah*!'

Everybody takes a deep breath and the look of bewilderment fades from all our faces. Even Sifra smiles a little and sits herself down for a moment, exhausted from her exertions. We write the word down, slowly copying from the blackboard, and translate it into our different languages. But Sifra does not give us much time to relax. She stands up again and writes down the word 'doctor' next to the word 'strike'. Another vivid display of movement designed to explain the word 'doctor' takes place. Poor Sifra, she must be at her wits' end; no wonder she is in such a bad mood. This time the Polish professor and Mr Katz are happy to oblige: they know the word *roffe* and inform us all in whispers. Lionel says nothing; he gives me furtive looks - he definitely fancies me. I feel a stirring, too. It has been such a long time. Quite disturbing.

'Doctor's strike? Unheard of. Such a thing could never happen in Romania!' Adele is quite vexed. She manages to express her disagreement.

They are striking for more money, better pay,' Sifra says, explaining each word. 'Doctors have rights.'

Lionel says in Romanian, frowning: 'They should be brought to order!'

Even I think that this is a step too far. They have the freedom to do so. Perhaps they have the right, but have they got no conscience? What about the people in need of care? Strange things happen in this new world.

The lesson finishes with a song: Ava Naghilah. We have already learned the words; it is part of our integration process.

The afternoon is free. After lunch we have to do homework and meet the other inmates. It is a little difficult to communicate but it is getting better, although the general tendency is to gravitate around the people with whom we share a mother tongue. They are lovely people, each one trying to adapt to this new life.

Mr Katz is a tailor and his wife a housewife. They lived in the town of Roman all their lives. They were happy there and still miss the lovely park surrounded by old chestnut and oak trees. But they came here so that their children could have a future. They have two teenage sons who have made rapid language progress and are now at school, mixing with their new friends. Mr Katz hopes to open a shop soon after the Ulpan. He has set his heart on the town of Beersheba, the capital of the Negev, the ancient Judea. He is a serious man, with little schooling, and he struggles to learn. But he knows that he will need basic language knowledge to be able to communicate with customers. His wife appears more able than he is. She has to learn administrative skills besides the basic language and she is anxious to be able to do so. She is a lovely motherly type, who seems to take the whole world under her wing. She appears to want to extend her wing over me as well but I don't feel the need for mothering.

Adele seems very nice. She is single; she informs us that she is a divorcee of long standing and that she has a grown-up daughter. It is not clear whether the daughter is still in Romania or if they have come together. She seems to seek my friendship and I am glad; we are both a bit lonely. The two of us and Lionel are the only single people in the group.

One evening, after a few glasses of Israeli sweet wine, tongues loosen. Adele confides in us: 'Life has not been the same for me since the death of Stalin, our mentor, our true leader.'

What? I am stunned! 'How come?' I ask, when I recover from the shock.

'I lost all faith in communism with the attitude of the new leaders,' she says and I can see, to my surprise, that Lionel is nodding his head in agreement with her words.

'I was a member of the Party for a long time. The Party saw me through education, a right which I never had before,' she continues.

Aha! She is one of those who came from the workers' ranks, rushed through intensive schooling and put in a position of trust at the top of the pyramid. I hope she is and was a little more human than the nasty lot we had at med school, who came from the same pool. My blood starts boiling, but I want to hear more.

'After Stalin's death, we - the faithful, who had done so much to improve people's lives - were treated badly by the new leaders. I worked so hard for the publishing house Skintea, and I was demoted. That was unacceptable,' she adds.

'Were you a journalist?' I ask.

'No, I was a worker in the printing room before the socialist order came to power. I was chosen from the ranks and became the manager of the printing section, and when I put that in order and got rid of all the subversive characters, I was promoted as director of personnel.'

I can barely contain my anger. These were the people who ruled with an iron fist and caused harm to so many. The minute they lost their positions, they remembered that they had a family in Israel. I bet she kept that a secret; it would not have done her career prospects any good. I manage to say nothing. An artificial grin stays stuck on my lips. This is

Israel: every Jew has a right to come back to it. She, like me, came to visit relatives and never returned. I am no longer so sure that I want her as a friend. What a strange bunch we all are! I will have to be a little more careful about what I tell the others about myself.

12
THE NEW TOWN IN THE DESERT

The windows at the Ulpan do not open. Through the glass from my first-floor window I look out at the only view I have: slabs of grey concrete arranged in blocks of three or four storeys. The smooth monotony is interrupted by stairways placed at equal distances. Each flight of steps opens into a long continuous balcony before progressing to the next level. In between two stairways is the same number of doors. The doors stand like sentinels at equal distances, upright and immobile behind the balcony, guarding and defining each flat that is someone's home.

The blocks of flats are placed around a square built from the same materials, the concrete bleached white by the strong sun. In the square, children are playing football. From time to time a child screams loudly: '*Ima!*' The sound reverberates and ricochets against the solid walls. After a time and repeated calls, a woman appears on the balcony and a conversation starts, carried on the wings of the sound over two or three floors. Then the woman throws down the piece of clothing that the child has asked for or that the mother is making him wear.

On the balcony below, another woman puts the laundry out on a string fixed to the walls along the length of her flat. She listens to the conversation between the mother and the child and butts in with unsolicited advice. An elderly man from the floor below has something to say as well. The laundry blows in the wind. The gentle hot wind charged with red dust will dry it out quickly and lend a little colour to the white.

In the distance, the noise of building works overtakes the racket taking place down in the square. The children have loud voices; they speak even louder, and they carry on with conversations among themselves and through the air.

The red dust brought by the hot winds settles in the corners of the square and in peaks at the entrance steps of the stairways.

For some reason I think of snow. Snow drifts... Dan with a knitted scarf over his hat pulls a little sledge up and down our courtyard, thick with snow. Nicky, our niece Dana and Angela their friend take turns to ride amid shrieks of laughter.

After lunch we decide to take a walk to become familiar with and observe more of this little town. In Rome, I saw everything and perceived nothing, as though my eyes were closed. It will be different here.

Behind the Ulpan, part of the recently built estate, are rows of large metal refuse containers overflowing with thrown-out food. A few Arab women rummage through them, battling their way against the feral cats. A tarmac road stretches in front of us, covered like everything else in reddish powder dust that obliterates the edge markings. On our left there is a park laid out for recreation. Young palm trees are planted at equal distances, their spindly palm fingers yellow and grey. At the far end of the park, the old (well, older) part of town begins with a row of smaller two-storey blocks of flats. Each block wears an orange belt of gas tanks from which tubes emerge and creep upwards like serpents into each flat. There is a large central square which finally resembles an inhabited town centre. There is a patisserie displaying appetising cakes and savouries. A few men are sitting around, drinking coffee. Some of them wear civilian clothes, while others are in army fatigues. They are speaking so loudly that one may be forgiven for thinking that there are hundreds of them about. Some are white-skinned with ginger hair but others have darker complexions. Further on, we come across a shop - a supermarket - which sells everything: bread, milk, cheese, cakes, biscuits, tins, jars and fresh fruit. Women dressed in saris buy rice. Plump women with their heads covered with black kerchiefs carry baskets and shuffle their feet in slippers. Elderly Indian men wear fur hats. Young soldiers in army fatigues prop their tired heads on their army packs. There is a barber and a hairdresser, and a bar set above a large refrigeration counter displaying various salads. On a corner of the bar there is an electric grill. Pitta breads are grilled and then filled with a choice of salads, chickpea falafels and other vegetables that are totally unknown to me. Maybe I will try them out one day. People come and go, and take them away. A cream-coloured bus stops nearby and a group of youngish people - men and women wearing shorts, flip-flops on their feet and scanty vests or T-shirts - descend. These are the skilled people who work at the nuclear facility outside the town, returning home after the day's work. On the other side of the park there are a few rows of bungalows with little forecourts. We are told that they belong to some older better-off settlers, to the top leaders of the two factories attached to the town, Sivey and Kitan Dimona, or to the employees of the nuclear reactor, whose name is only whispered. There is a cinema advertising Indian films, we gather by the posters. We cannot read the titles. We walk back on the other side of the park.

The park is empty; a few branches of the palms, torn by the wind or by the children, lie on the ground. It looks like a desert island. It could be an oasis in the desert if there were water here. However, people - scientists, physicists and chemists - live here, engaged in the modern age sciences. We are told by someone that this is the safest place in Israel; nobody dares to bomb this place.

We return to the Ulpan and have a few glasses of wine in my flat, which is bigger. I am a doctor so I have privileges. We talk about our plans for the future, what we will do after we finish here. Adele says that she has relatives in Tel Aviv and that she hopes to find employment, through connections, at a publishing house. Lionel, who is single - divorced - tells us that he has been married three times before, but he was unlucky; three women left him. He does not elaborate. Instead, he makes plans for the future: before the war his father had a small factory making brushes. Since early childhood, he was brought up to know about different kinds of brushes, and hair and bristles from different animals. Some of his father's old apprentices have a business in Tel Aviv and he has been invited to join them. The Katzes have set their hearts on Beersheba. It is my turn to speak of the future. But I tell them that my future is on hold: I will not know till my family is here with me. I suppose I will find some work wherever there is a vacancy. Surely, they all protest, I have to make some plans; otherwise, I will end up in this shit-hole. So what? For me, if I am alone, it will not matter.

It is getting late. They all say goodbye: Adele and the Katzes - only Lionel stays a while longer to finish his drink. We sit for a moment, both with our own thoughts. Then he puts his large arm round my shoulder and I find it soothing. I lean against him for comfort. What follows is a long, passionate night; we cling to each other, like two desperate beings, all doubts drowned in the animal, primitive, rough sex. No emotion, no thought - just an anchor, clinging to life. Exhausted, we sleep.

What follows, when we wake up, is a reluctance to acknowledge the day and an exchange of apologies; he for taking advantage, me for being weak. We avoid looking at each other, get dressed and he hurries to his rooms. Soon it will be time for lessons and Sifra is not one to be kept waiting!

13
A DECENT PROPOSAL

Lionel is very tall and heavily built. He walks with a slight stoop, as if embarrassed by his height. His manner is shy and he needs a lot of encouragement to talk. He wears glasses and does not look people in the eyes. His hair is cropped short, military fashion, and he is clean-shaven. He exudes a quiet power. He said he was a colonel in the army, and I still vaguely wonder why he is here, especially after I saw him agreeing with Adele. Is he also one of the Stalinist escapees who fell out of grace with the new communist lot?

But I must not dwell on this matter; it does not really concern me. All I know is that he is lovely in bed: considerate, powerful and intent on giving me pleasure. That is all I need to keep my strength and draw comfort. Lionel has plans to start a small brush factory like his father before him. That's fine by me, as long as he makes no demands. He keeps asking me to go with him and marry him. I keep repeating that I am already married. I know I do not love him. Why can't people leave things be?

One lunchtime, near my birthday, Haike, the school administrator, comes in and seats herself at my table. She has all the makings of an efficient administrator - don't ask me why; I cannot define it.

She exudes power and I am fearful of power. Her hair is straight, dyed red.

'You're a doctor, I hear?' she starts, as though she's preparing for a long conversation.

I sigh, 'Yes, I am a doctor.'

'What kind of a doctor?' She does not look at me and instead just plays with an empty glass, twisting it round and round.

'I am a family medicine doctor, although I've worked in a hospital for the last few years.' There is a long pause. Haike settles in her seat and carries on turning that glass. Neither of us speaks for a while.

'I was asked by someone from the polyclinic, Kupat Holim we call it, whether there is a doctor among the new group of students here in residence. Looking through the files, I thought you might be interested. Anyway, I told the man that I would look into it.'

I am taken aback. I stop eating and put my fork down; I don't know what to say.

'My language is not good enough to express and hold an argument; it is too soon!' I say and I am trying desperately to keep calm.

'That doesn't matter too much,' Haike says and takes another sip of her drink. I look at her more closely; she is middle-aged and has a large mouth, a strong jaw and thin lips. Her red hair flies everywhere; she has something Russian about her.

I am annoyed because I feel that I am stammering. 'But I have no papers to prove who I am and what qualifications I hold—'

'This can be arranged,' she interrupts me mid-sentence. 'Do you have any colleagues, friends or relatives here who could testify that they know you? Besides, it was written in your passport.' How does she know what's on my passport?

Another long pause. She puts her elbows on the table in a resolute business-like manner. 'Look, there is a strike on! People need a doctor; the staff are overwhelmed and say they cannot cope any longer. I was asked to put a name forward, even for a short while. If you could cover for the doctors on strike, formalities could be started and whatever else needs to be done to make it all legal. That is, if you would like to continue afterwards in Dimona.'

'Can I think about it?' I ask in a small voice.

'Don't take too long. Come to my office this afternoon.' She leaves with a curt goodbye.

I stand to leave as well, my appetite gone, and I don't know what to do. I need to talk it over with someone. But who? Lionel would be no help; he wants me to go with him to Tel Aviv. My uncles would say the same as before: 'Do what you feel is right.'

Here I go again: decisions, situations thrown at me and I am not prepared for any of this. It would have been nice to start what I thought would be a normal life. I was hoping that after improving my language skills, I would attend some courses to learn at least the names of medicines used in this country. How will I understand my patients, write a letter to a colleague or even find the confidence to prescribe? I need to get hold of some books or information leaflets, also borrow some money and speak to some of my colleagues. I will see if someone will help me to find their addresses in a telephone directory, as it is all in Hebrew. That is, if I accept the offer. I am scared; I do not think I can cope. Yet again, I am being thrown in at the deep end. Everybody knows what I should do and I know that I am not ready. I have not yet fully recovered from my Italian adventure and I have to start work without proper language skills, and no knowledge of the organisation, the people and the array of medicines available. But a refusal may be considered a bad mark on my CV. And I could do with some money... Besides being a defector and an immigrant, I would now be a 'black leg', as people who break a strike are called - or so I had read in novels. However, I believe that doctors shouldn't strike.

I go to my room. In a sulk I climb into my bed, cover my head and lie there. Perhaps this is the way my life's pathway is set: falling into situations that an invisible hand has set out for me. What will I say? What is there to do? I will do as I always do: as I am told.

14
BACK TO WORK

It is nearly the end of the day. Time to telephone my old friends.

Katy is a chemist. Her family emigrated many years ago and she has made quite a reputation for herself as an industrial chemist. I was told that she even has her own brand of lipstick and creams. She sounds pleased to hear from me and starts reminiscing about our little adventures in our student days, but my coins are running out fast. I ask her what I should do and she says that I should get out of Dimona because once I start working, they will not let me go; it will not be a good career move. With the remaining coins, I ring Mady at the shop. She is her usual self, warm and friendly, and she returns the call to give me the contact numbers of some of the people I grew up with in Focsani. Davy, one of my friends, says that I should take the job, to hell with the strike; He is a dentist and continues to work although many of his colleagues have joined the strike. I ring my childhood friend Edith. She is a doctor practising at a hospital in Tel Aviv. She left Romania ten years earlier, soon after graduation. We used to see each other during our med school years. She was a year above me and once we were sent to work in different parts of the country, we lost touch. She sounds all formal and distant. She asks what on earth I am doing there, at the back of beyond! I don't know what I am doing here, but I don't tell her that.

Later still I speak to Abraham, who has already heard the story from his wife.

'Do what your heart and mind tell you to do,' he answers. 'Don't you know that no matter how many Jews you ask the same question, each will give you a different answer and insist that you should take only their advice, because each of them knows best? That is why we have 16 political parties and we are only three million people.'

OK, Myra, I say to myself, *after all, it is up to you. It will be for a short while only, till the end of this strike. It will give you an insight into how things work round here, what it is to practise your chosen profession here. You may actually learn something. It's a good opportunity and you will get money! You will not have to borrow from your relatives and you will be able to afford the weekly fares to Jerusalem.* Because that is what I have been doing up till now. Sunday mornings I'd skip lessons and take the train from Dimona to Jerusalem. In Jerusalem I'd walk to the Parliament building, the Knesset, alone - or sometimes with Lionel for company - and ask to speak to the secretary who is dealing with my case. Sometimes he will see me and other times, which is more often the case, he will not. I wait for hours and Lionel waits with me, and I am pleased to have his company. At the same time I hate him for wishing that I won't succeed, which I can read in his eyes. On occasions, the secretary finds a few seconds to see me and replies to my one and only question saying: 'Patience, *Savlanut*! *Yhie tov*! All will be well,' and he taps me on the shoulder reassuringly.

I come out none the wiser and Lionel jokes: 'If he carries on like that, you will end up with a dropped shoulder!'

Ha ha! It's easy for him to joke. He is single and he hopes we will become an item, although I have told him that this cannot be. For me it is important to keep the pressure up and the hope alive if I am to see my child again.

Back at the Ulpan we end the day in my room and make love with the intensity of a soothing balm on an open wound.

The question that remains is: how would I make myself understood and how would I offer people, assuming any of them would want to see me, the best of care?

The day following my conversation with Haike I decide to skip school again and walk to the polyclinic. It is a fairly new building, like everything else here, large and with a wide, clean entrance hall like any institution. I approach the desk and introduce myself. The woman behind the desk immediately rings through for the administrator. He is a young man, all smiles.

'No problem. It's going to be all right; we are glad to have you.' My questions about medicines are answered in the same way: no problem - *ein bayah*! The local pharmacist is a Romanian and he will help; all will be well!

He introduces me to the nurses next. One young woman is from Morocco and the other, more mature one, is from Russia. They are very eager for me to join them. I ask about the nearest hospital, transport and who should be contacted in an emergency. 'No problem,' the administrator says. He will be at hand should the need arise and the nurses hasten to promise their help as well.

It occurs to me that life is simple here. This does not entirely calm my anxieties. It seems that all is too easy; everything is no problem - *ein bayah.*

15
THE PATIENTS

Here I am, in my office. The white coat, like a skin that peels off my anxiety and makes it vanish, is on. In this environment, I know who I am: I am in charge! When I enter the building, the receptionist hastens to say good morning with a big smile. He speaks slowly, careful to make sure I understand, and informs me of the day's problems. I nod knowingly to make a good impression and turn my once again confident steps towards the office. People come; they speak Russian, French, Hebrew, English and Romanian. Jacqueline, the nurse, is at hand for instant translations and so is Ludmila, the elderly Russian. My prescriptions are as long as a love letter, written in Romanian longhand to the ever obliging pharmacist. I write a generic name and explain why I chose it. For example: 'I don't know what is the name you use here but I wish to prescribe a painkiller in a simple compound. This patient has allergies and a stomach ulcer, so no aspirin.' Also, 'This patient has an irregular heartbeat. I need a beta blocker. Please choose a non-specific one; this patient has asthma and let me know as well what you call this product.' Or, 'This elderly woman needs a cough mixture but she has high blood pressure. Please, is there a preparation without ephedrine? What is it called?'

The reply comes without fail, and the pharmacist is proud to be given a choice and to be fully informed. And he sends me leaflets with information in English and French, which I struggle to memorise. What's more, he spreads the word to whoever he meets at the pharmacy about what a good, honest and knowledgeable doctor has been bestowed upon Dimona! As a result, the queues to see me become longer. There is no appointment system in place so I, eager to prove myself, work long hours, till I have seen all the people waiting. I have some problems with writing medical certificates, but the administrator fills that job for me, when I tell him to. Within a week or two everybody is my friend. I seem to have aroused a lot of curiosity in town. Some of the ladies who represent the elite of the community put in an appearance, asking to have their blood pressure taken and if I know of any new remedies for aging skin. 'The sun is so damaging! Lines grow on faces like mushrooms.'

I wish I knew the answers. I am flattered, particularly when I am invited to join one little private party or another. At the parties they try to draw me into medical advice conversations and I do my best to avoid giving offence but I ask them to come and see me individually at the polyclinic after hours, so that we will have more time to talk. Yet, they are scared that they will offend their previous doctors and want to be in good terms with both, just in case.

At the office, the people seeking advice seem to be predominantly European; I learn, like everybody here, to refer to them by the country they came from, forgetting the fact that we are all of the same ethnicity. I learn gradually that the Romanians and Russians tend to be more dramatic. A lot of them worry about small things but like to be reassured; they do not like bad news spelt out and when something wrong happens, their first reaction is to deny it, blame it on someone, more often the doctor, or seek a second opinion.

I hear hard words from the Goldsteins, who brought their daughter, Fanny, because she is vomiting. After all my advice, she continues to vomit the next day and the day after that, and they start shouting at me, the father banging my desk: 'Do something! All you doctors are useless!'

I look down and notice that the girl, who is nine years old, is unsteady on her feet. I ask her to count her fingers and she misses. Each time she misses the target. In that split second I realise that this is serious. I need to examine her properly. 'I think I would like to send you to Beersheba to see a neurologist, a brain doctor,' I say.

'What are you talking about? Can't you treat even an indigestion?'

The mother starts crying: 'There's nothing the matter with my child's brain! What are you saying? She is the first in her class! She is good at everything! Morris, let's leave! We'll find a proper doctor.'

'Wait, please! This could be serious. Please let me write to the neurologist or I could telephone him – it is important. Perhaps it's nothing, but it is better to know.'

They relent but the mother is still crying and she darts venomous looks towards me. I examine the child and curse myself for taking it so lightly three days ago, but you don't suspect a brain tumour each time someone comes in with vomiting.

The father stands up and says, 'We don't need your referral. We have family in Tel Aviv and with their help we shall go to the best specialist. Privately!' With that, they leave muttering a mumbled goodbye. I feel shaken, so unsure of myself, and even question what I have seen. Three or four weeks later I hear from them again. The Goldsteins request a home visit. By that time another doctor has returned to work, and I ask the administrator to inform the family, as they may not want me to visit. They insist. They specifically requested me, I am told. The girl is out of hospital and the operation went well. Although she is smiling, the mother has deep hollows round her eyes and tears running down her nose. She greets me at the door and hugs me. 'Thank you, thank you,' she says. I feel happy for them, and glad that they have forgiven me, but deep down, I feel that I had failed.

Not long after, the Moroccan Rabbi comes and asks to see a doctor. No, the matter can't wait. I am the only one around and I receive him. He says in French that this morning, when he arrived and unlocked the synagogue door, he found a little child asleep on the floor. The child is so frightened and refuses to speak, and the Rabbi does not know whose family he belongs to. He would like me to come and examine the child to make sure that he has not damaged himself, the way he thrashes about. Jacqueline, the nurse, wants to come with us. She knows most of the families originating from Morocco and she may recognise the child.

We arrive at the place and find that the four- or five-year-old child is very frightened but, as far as I can tell, is all right. Jacqueline thinks that she knows the family; she remembers that they have many children. We arrive at their house and are met by the father. He immediately picks up the child and the child seems happy.

'Thank you so much, Rabbi,' he says. 'Last night, after the service, was the only night I forgot to count them before they went to bed.' The family has 14 children. When I return to the Ulpan, I must tell them the story.

16
THE TROUBLE WITH SIFRA

On a Thursday morning, as I come in, I am told that there is an emergency waiting. I rush to my office and there she is: Sifra, larger than ever. I have not seen her for some time; my new all-absorbing job has not left me much time for Hebrew lessons. Besides, Lionel told me that Ora, a young teacher who is completing her conscription service, is taking the lessons of late.

Sifra is pacing up and down the small waiting room, her face set and distorted with fury or pain, I cannot tell which. I say hello and open the door. She marches in without a greeting and shouts, 'My tummy hurts!'

My old timid anxiety threatens to invade me: 'Please lie down on the couch and I will examine you.' I try to control my voice from shaking.

Without a word she climbs on the couch, her feet dangling over. She is taller than the length of the couch and her abdomen is enormous, tight as a drum. *Good God,* I think. *She is with child.*

What is the date of delivery? (I don't know the word for delivery). 'Are you due now?' I ask.

'What is due? What are you talking about?' she replies. 'Just do your job. Examine me and give me something for the pain. I cannot bear it, hurry up!'

I feel I cannot trust myself; perhaps I am wrong. I think I am going to stutter. I touch her belly and I listen to it with my steth. There is a baby in there, unless it is an enormous tumour or I am dreaming and this is not happening. Another opinion would be handy but there is no other medic around.

'When was your last period?' I stammer.

'What is it to you? That's none of your business! This is very intrusive! I am never regular,' she says after a while.

Now I am really stammering and new words fail me. 'A baby is coming.'

'*Stouyot*! Rubbish!' Her face contorts as another wave of pain grips her. 'You call yourself a doctor?! Give me something for the pain! What sort of doctor are you?' Her screams bring Jaqueline rushing in.

'I don't think a painkiller will help.'

Jaqueline assesses the situation and says, 'I am going to ring for an ambulance.'

'I don't need an ambulance,' Sifra shouts. She gets up, pulls her trousers up and storms out of the room. Both nurses are now in my room, looking as stunned as I am. I tell them that this woman is in labour but she maintains that she has never had sex with anyone and therefore it is impossible for her to have a baby. They saw her when she left screaming. They both say, 'Well, that's her problem. If she doesn't want an ambulance, let her have the baby in the sand.'

I insist and ask Jacqueline to go ahead and ask for the ambulance to come to the Ulpan.

In the meantime, people are waiting outside and I need to start my consultations. I cannot concentrate – Sifra is on my mind. Not long after, the telephone rings: it is Haike, the Ulpan administrator. My heart misses a beat.

'Sifra delivered a baby. In the toilet. As soon as she arrived. Good job the ambulance came within minutes. They had to sedate and restrain her to take her away.'

I am mortified. 'I tried to keep her here and send for the ambulance. Is the baby alive?' I ask.

'Yes, it's a girl: black as coal,' Haike giggles.

I think I am going to faint and I lean heavily on the desk for support

I don't know how I am going to get through the afternoon. At lunch I don't show my face in the dining room. I think people will have heard the story and laugh at me. They will say that I cannot deal with a pregnant woman, that I put her and her child's life in danger. I am going through the sequence of events again and again: what could I have done differently? I should have run after her… I should have asked the nurses to go after her… I don't know. Perhaps if I had been less scared of her as my teacher, I would have been more assertive. If I were fluent in Hebrew, I could have had a talk with the hospital specialist, and also been able to calm her down and reason with her. I don't know. I don't think I am any good. I might as well join Lionel and learn how to make brushes. Give it all up.

I return to the surgery and sleepwalk through the consultations with my patients. At around 5 o'clock in the afternoon Ora turns up at the surgery.

'Sifra is creating havoc at the hospital. She does not want to have any care from the staff. She is still in denial; she does not want to see the baby. She says that she will only speak to you. I have a car so can we go when you finish here?'

Of course I can, since it is all my responsibility. The thought of the reception I will get from the hospital staff makes me wish I were ill and could not move.

At the maternity hospital we meet the nurse in charge and ask for Sifra by name.

'Ah, *Mariam a kdoshah*, Holy Mary the virgin,' she says and directs us to her. I didn't expect that the nurses would take it so lightly. It seems that everybody knows about her and calls her either Holy Mary or Virgin Mary. She is lying on her side, facing the wall. Ora starts speaking to her softly. Sifra turns and, pointing towards me, shouts, 'I don't want to speak to you, only to her! She is responsible!' At that moment, I feel so sorry for this woman who still lives in denial and I feel I should have done more to help her. If only I had known her better; if only I had understood. She needs help, not people making fun of her.

So Ora leaves me alone with Sifra. I shudder at what is coming: I can hear the nurses hovering in the background, obviously to be at hand should the need arise.

'I am going to sue you! You put my life in danger,' she says, her eyes blazing. I think I understand what she is saying, but I am not sure. My heart jumps in my chest.

'Yes,' she continues. 'Negligence! Failure in your duty! Why did you not help me?'

I cannot speak. I don't know what to say.

'But I won't. Instead, you need to do something for me,' she says. 'Have you got a pen?' I fumble in my bag with shaking hands and produce a pen and a notebook.

'Write down this number and ask for—' and she gives me a name. 'Ring and explain. They will help me to come out of this nightmare.' With that she turns her face to the wall. I leave without a single word having passed my lips. I breathe fast and the pulse is pounding in my ears. I would have loved to hold her hand and reassure her, and offer my help but I can't do it. Slowly, I recover my composure. I will ring; I would like to prepare a speech, as I think that the number must be her parents'. I go outside and talk to Ora, and I beg her to ring on my behalf. I cannot say much in Hebrew or English. That is what we do; we return to the Ulpan and I tell Ora what she has to say. She dials the number and a formal, well-spoken English female voice informs us that the person we named is no longer an active member of the Embassy. He was recalled a few days earlier. She asks us not to use this number again.

This was the last I heard from Sifra. Some time later I got news from the hospital that the baby girl was successfully adopted. I am sure I will carry the guilt for the rest of my life.

17
CITIZEN OF DIMONA

Here I am: I become a citizen of Dimona. I sign a contract with the polyclinic and am elevated overnight to the professional elite of the town. I find friends among the residents. I suspect it's because it is useful to be friends with a doctor but I like to think that they also like me a little.

Within weeks I am given a private apartment. Housing is provided for all newcomers, especially in the new towns. Mine is on the first floor, near the centre of the town and not far from my office. The apartment comes with a single iron-framed bed, a table and two chairs, a mop and bucket, and a single-ring gas hob - courtesy of the Immigration Agency. The apartment is composed of two bedrooms, one slightly larger than the other, and a small sitting room which opens on to a balcony. The windows are all fitted with standard plastic venetian blinds. There are a shower and a toilet in the bathroom, which also houses a large water tank. The kitchen is small, with a few white plastic units, a sink and the hob. This is the height of luxury for me. It is my first own home! The following Saturday my uncles come bearing gifts: bedding, crockery and cutlery to give me a start in life. I feel like a newlywed.

It is the end of the month and I receive my first salary. I have done a few night duties, which are paid double, and as a new immigrant, I am exempt from taxes for three years. I can't wait to get the money so I can go and buy a sofa and two easy chairs like the ones my new friends have in their sitting room, and also a double bed and bedside tables. I will move the single bed in the little room. That will be Nicky's bed. I will get a wardrobe for her, and a small desk and chair.

What I also need is a fridge. My uncle Leon offers to order one from abroad - he is dealing in import/export for the new immigrants - but I rather like the large fridge-freezers like Mady has and they are made locally. Payday arrives and I get a long narrow statement with lots of writing on it which I find hard to decipher, but where is the money? Later in the day I receive a visit from the local bank manager. He came out of courtesy, he says, to advise me to open a bank account. He explains that this way my salary will go directly into my account. I feel almost threatened or cheated: they do not want to give me my money. They want to use my money under the pretext of doing it for my own safety, for my own good. But I do not trust him or his bank. I am used to seeing the colour of my money. I don't understand all this talk about accounts and I insist that I want what is owed to me, in cash. The man looks puzzled but refrains from making any further comment. He leaves and when he returns half an hour later, he hands me a fairly large packet of crisp notes. He is still wearing a suspicious look and I think I've done the right thing: these banks want to get hold of my money and use it the way they like. I know better than to play their game! I relax and start making plans.

The next day is a Saturday and I make a trip to Beersheba, as arranged with my cousin Amnon, to visit a few large furniture stores.

We arrive fairly late but the furniture store that I was advised to go to is still open. There is a large selection of everything in every colour: mostly straight lines, Ercol furniture, pine and Formica. I make my selection, and feel so happy that I can afford it and still have a little left over. I open my bag and start counting. Halfway through my counting, the owner of the business comes in and interrupts me.

'No, please,' he says. 'I don't take cash. Cheques only and not the whole sum. Give me ten cheques, dated one a month for the next ten months.' I stop dead. He does not want my money! He is prepared to send over all that I've ordered on a promise. He wants cheques and he explains that paying over ten months is better for his taxes. I never heard such a thing in my life! Certainly not in Romania! I don't have a chequebook; I refused to have one. I must learn to trust the banks with my earnings. I return to my flat and first thing on Monday morning, I go to the bank and open an account. Whatever he thought of all that, the bank manager does not make any reference to it or to our previous encounter. I feel like a peasant who has come to town for the first time.

18
7 JULY 1970

I love my home. Every morning I wake up and it is so quiet. It begins to look homely with the new furniture, curtains and light fittings. Nicky's room has curtains, besides the customary blinds. I have painted the single bed given to me when I moved in so now it is white and pink, and the spread tells the story of Snow White. I hope she will like it when she arrives. I don't know when that will be, but I am sure that she will. I've ordered some carpets so the floors won't look bare.

Lionel came to visit but I felt that I did not wish him to intrude into my home, my family home. We met at the restaurant in the commercial centre. He was upset and I felt sorry for him but I tried to explain that what happened at the Ulpan belonged to a time there - a time of sweet memories - and we have moved on from it. We meet a few more times on my regular visits to Jerusalem and then we drift apart.

I see patients every day; they keep me busy. I go to Beersheba once a week for some tutorials. The specialist in internal medicine is German; he is a charming elderly man who is very skilled and very precise in his manner, and direct in his dealings with the patients. He treats us, new immigrant doctors, with courtesy and respect. However, he is less gracious with the Palestinian student attached to his team. I notice that the young man, with curly black hair, almost shakes when the consultant addresses him in a commanding tone, and he hastens to fulfil every task that the consultant gives him, but he never gets a thank you in reply.

My colleagues at Dimona Kupat Holim are friendly but reserved. One is from Argentina, the other is from Romania and the director is an Israeli of the second generation. He was trained at Hadassa Hospital and is a paediatrician. None of them is keen to do night duties, but I am happy to do as many nights as possible; the pay is good and I don't sleep much anyway. Once in a while, I have a weekend to myself to recover my strength.

On such an evening in July, I am off duty, free to recover. It is so hot that I toss and turn, allowing the sheet to cool under me. I get up and have another shower. I watch the clock: it is 3 a.m. and I wonder if I will get any sleep at all and how I will feel tomorrow when I am back at work.

My doorbell starts ringing – not once or twice but several times, its shrill sound piercing the dark and hurting my ears. Who could it be, at this hour? It must be an emergency, a patient who did not read the list displayed at the polyclinic, at the pharmacy and on the town hall's windows. I am not going to open the door; whoever is there will finally realise and go somewhere else. He or she will eventually find the right person. The ringing continues and I can also hear voices, men's voices, down in the street. I refuse to budge. If I do it now, this will become a habit: everyone will disturb the doctor who is nearest to where they live and none of us will get any rest or a break. We are human after all.

While I am debating all these arguments with myself, I can hear that someone is turning the key to unlock my door. My God, now I am frightened! I hasten to put on a nightie. The only person who has a key to my apartment is my next-door neighbour, Madame Ben-Harosh. But, why is she coming in at this hour? Or, could it be a burglar who has master keys?

'Myra, Myra!' I hear Madame Ben-Harosh's loud voice and I think that she is crying. 'Myra, your family is here!'

My family. Which family is she talking about?

'Your husband and your daughter are here!'

I move a few steps along the corridor, uncomprehending. I can't believe my eyes: Dan is standing behind my neighbour with Nicky asleep in his arms. I cannot move; I cannot breathe. My head is empty and I cannot speak.

'Why didn't you come to greet us at the airport? Didn't you receive my telegram?' An anxious, tired and unshaven Dan approaches and gives me a kiss on the cheek.

I shake my head. Behind Dan I see some men in army uniform. They say, 'Right, we found her. Time to go back.' My neighbour and her husband, who by now have joined the party, shake hands with the men. They say goodbye to Dan and I do nothing, just stay there propped up against the cool corridor wall.

Dan asks where he should put Nicky down. At that I stir and guide them to the small bedroom, where the bed has been ready to receive my precious gift ever since I moved in. We finally embrace and our silent tears mix with our kisses. Dan shows me the stub of the telegram he sent that morning – the telegram that never arrived or perhaps was never sent by the bored, envious clerk at the Bucharest post office. I shudder when I think of Dan and Nicky arriving on a night flight, and the Immigration Agency people asking him all the questions, checking his entrance papers and asking if anyone was there to greet them. He would have answered yes to that; he would have shown the stub of the telegram that he had sent. 'Let's wait, my wife will be here soon,' but a few hours later the people on duty must have looked at him – suspiciously or concerned, I don't know which – and noticed how bewildered and tired the two of them looked. So they decided to put their belongings on a truck and drive through the night to Dimona, not knowing whether there was a wife there or not.

This must be one of the cruellest events in our lives. Nicky asking: where is Mummy? Does Mummy not want us? I don't think I will ever forget it.

The next day I telephone the polyclinic to let them know that I will not come in and they will have to make do without me. I have to watch over my two arrivals, my two gifts who turned up entirely unexpectedly, when I had nearly lost hope and convinced myself that I should try to learn to live without them. They are asleep now but soon, when they wake up, together, we will telephone our family. Then, I will take them by the hand and show them to my friends.

19
TOGETHER WE SETTLE IN

That is what I do. Sanda and Harry, Zitta and Nutty, Viorel and Viorica, the colleagues at the polyclinic and Haike at the Ulpan - everyone is moved to tears. They hug Dan and kiss Nicky; everybody hastens to receive us and give a party. Nicky loves all the attention, kisses and presents. The whole town rejoices; the party mood prevails. As for me, I am not sure I am all there: I am not listening to people talking. I walk in a dream, squeezing Nicky's hand and touching her as if to reassure myself that she is real. I take a week off work.

One week to get together; so much has happened in the last 18 months that we feel the need to reconnect. Nicky has grown so much: her golden hair is long, and she is lively and chatty. Dan is his usual quiet self: I have to ask a lot of questions to get any news of the ones left behind. Nicky tells me that her cousin Daniela has started school and can write, whereas she did not fancy learning all that Mammy tried to teach her. She loves playing and games, and she can't wait to meet the new friends she has already made in Dimona.

She does not mention the grandparents. She wets the bed almost every night.

We take another week and spend it in a kibbutz near Jerusalem. We visit the town, Dan guiding us to all the places that he remembers from his early years. He remembers the King David hotel, where he lived for a while, and he goes in search of the Romanian Orthodox church where he lived with his mother, father and Lydia till they were shipped to London. It is situated in the vicinity of the ultra-Orthodox Jewish quarter of Mea Sharim. Nicky keeps asking why those people wear black clothes and hats. Dan knows all the streets in the old town, and we visit churches and shops with wonderful objects kept by Greeks shopkeepers. We drink coffee brought on copper trays in minute cups. We put a note of thanks in a crevice of the Wailing Wall.

We have a lovely time: we walk, we talk and Dan tells us stories of his childhood. On the way back home we stop to see the family in Tel Aviv, the uncles who receive us all with open arms. They are all so happy for us. Amnon introduces his friend Shula and announces that they will be getting married as soon as she finishes her Chemistry course at the technical college. His older brother Emmanuel and his wife Lyorah bring their newborn child for us to meet. Nicky is happy with all the cuddles and gifts, all eyes on her. Dan is cheerful, and he jokes and talks to everyone. I am happy; things are going well – it is a moment of happiness that I shall cherish for ever.

Nicky wants to know why her father knows the old city of Jerusalem and in the evening he starts telling her the story that I have heard so many times.

'When I was a little boy, I lived for a short while in this town. I don't remember much but the grand hotel King David was the best then, although it looks a little tired now. I remember eating at a grand table, all laid out beautifully. I was with my mum and dad, and my sister Lydia; she was three and I was nearly five. Then we lived at the Romanian Church house. I only remember sliding down the banisters of the old stone house. My father, your pappy, was a freedom fighter against the Nazis who befriended the Romanian Government, so we had to leave to save our lives. Once out of Romania, Pappy joined the Allied forces and we were sent to Jerusalem. That was long, long ago, before you were born.'

We return to Dimona. By that time, all the tearful and emotional visits had quietened down: my news is old news and almost forgotten, as life returns to its normal course.

Nicky gets to know the children in the neighbourhood. They do not speak the same language but that seems to be no barrier. They play in the street without fear. By September, when the time comes to start school, she speaks Hebrew almost well, but she does not want to go. Once she is in school, she often runs away or refuses to take part in lessons. The teacher is not concerned but I am. Every evening I ask her what happened at school and she replies lifting her shoulders in two brief successive movements – a gesture that she has recently acquired. 'Nothing. I don't remember.'

I ask if she has any homework, anything we can do together, and she says that she hasn't any. I do not have enough time to give her. The demands of my work are increasing. Dan starts looking for a job.

I suggest to Dan that he goes to the Ulpan as a daily student so that he can learn the language, but he feels reluctant to do so. He thinks that he will pick it up as he goes along and in the meantime he can manage with his English. He is more interested in passing his driving test and thinks that we should buy a car. He wants to find work and help his parents who were left behind. He makes a lot of friends. He can't stand the heat and he sleeps badly. That makes him a little irritable. Things are uneasy between us; lots of things remain unsaid. We both have to face the fact that something has changed and we are not the same people.

Dan is trying to regain the upper hand in our relationship but I am now, by force of circumstance, the main breadwinner, the most adapted and settled person in this place. I feel bad that he and Nicky are not entirely happy. I was foolish to think that everything would be instantly perfect. Like everything else in life, time is needed to smooth the edges. Our intimate encounters are lacking warmth. He thrusts himself into me, trying to assert himself, and I submit, the sense of my guilt - and perhaps his as well - unspoken and unresolved.

20
LET'S LIVE AGAIN

The atmosphere of wellbeing persists: new friends and new invitations, as if we have become suddenly very special, as if after Nicky and Dan's arrival we have become different. I am no longer seen as a single woman; my status has altered. We have climbed on a different scale of appreciation in the eyes of our peers and family. Nicky revels in all the attention. Family and friends make every effort to make us feel welcome and accepted. But I feel that there is too much fuss, too much effort to display affection which, in effect, singles us out and makes Dan feel different. Most of our new friends feel embarrassed when we listen to the news together. When the almost daily debate about who is a Jew and who is not a Jew takes place, everybody starts talking at once about different topics. When the English programme starts on television, discussing whether mixed-ethnicity soldiers should be buried in a Jewish cemetery, the persons present find themselves at a loss and stop talking. Dan grits his teeth and looks down, and the uneasy silence threatens to ruin the evening. It is usually at this point that Harry, or Nouty, proposes a game of American poker and the awkwardness fades into the background.

The Dimona mayor takes Dan under his wing. He makes a special effort to get him a good job. There is an offer for oil prospecting in the desert, which I thought would please Dan, as it is his specialty. But he refuses. He does not want to work in the heat of the desert. Indeed, the heat does not agree with him and he comes out in hives. He sleeps badly. Instead, following Harry's advice, he accepts a job in Yerucham, a town nearby. 'Now,' he says, 'we can buy a car. As soon as possible.' I cannot drive but he can, although he could not take his driving test in Bucharest, where you had to have a car to be permitted to take the test. We could not afford to buy a car. Now we can, and we get our first Fiat. Dan chooses a sports model, light blue. He passes the test and is the happiest he has been since his arrival. He drives fast, taking risks. It is as if he wants to prove something. I can't say I am enjoying the experience.

It seems to me that Harry and Sanda have appointed themselves as our protectors and advisors. They are old settlers who are by now comfortably off. They are good people and, not having children of their own, they have fallen in love with Nicky. As theirs is a mixed marriage, that is perhaps why Dan gravitates towards them and befriends them more than all the other couples who are our friends. Harry is an extrovert; he is big built, his voice is booming when he speaks and he enjoys an audience. The local gossip says that he has had several extramarital affairs. The most recent nearly ended their marriage, but each time Sanda takes him back after his profuse apologies and promises. Being in the same profession as Dan, Harry is assuming the role of mentor. He knows all there is to know about everyone and everything, and Dan follows. And little by little Sanda grows in Dan's eyes into the epitome of elegance and style, good taste and good manners. We become daily visitors to their house and Sanda takes care of Nicky when she comes back from school, if I am delayed. That pleases Dan but I don't know how I feel. I don't want to admit even to myself that I would prefer to be left alone so that my daughter and I could be getting to know each other a little better and let our love get stronger each day. Then I curse myself for harbouring such mean feelings.

I feel as if our lives have fractured and, like any fracture that is nurtured and fixed in plaster, given time, it will mend.

It mends but will never be the same as it was in the beginning. Although on the surface the appearance does not show any difference to the naked eye, the mending point starts hurting again after a while, much later, after the accident is almost forgotten.

One cannot measure time in seasons here. The sky is permanently blue, and it is hot. It's useless to look up to the sky in search of telltale clouds: it almost never rains. It can be monotonous and irritating. Every evening we go to Sanda's. She likes having people around and playing the part of the gracious hostess. She teaches Nicky good manners; Sanda has had them since childhood, taught strictly by her own mother. Her father was a member of the nobility who married the governess. That gives her the upper hand over all the others; she is the leader in good taste and most of her friends - us included - feel privileged to be accepted in her circle.

One day we are invited to dinner, and we accept gratefully. We are the only ones present. I think this is unusual and feel something different in the air. The conversation changes from the usual niceties to a more serious subject and I begin to understand why we are the only guests. Harry has received an offer to work in Germany for six months at an important factory. One of the businessmen who visited the Dimona factory, where Harry is the director, has written, inviting him to work at his factory in Gladbach.

He is eager to go, as he does not think that there is a future for him in Dimona. The local textile industry is nearly bankrupt. He talked it over with Sanda and they agreed that Harry should go alone, see how things develop and return home at the end of the contract to revise their plans. He asks us to look after Sanda while he is away. I stop to think, trying to take it all in, but Dan is eager and accepts immediately. What's more, Harry starts talking to Dan, saying, 'There is no hope we will grow old here. I look at you. You are like a fish out of water.' He touches Dan's shoulder. 'All those factories will sooner or later run out of steam. There is no market for what we produce, and with the war just following us like a shadow, there is little hope we could expand our markets.'

'I am all right here, but by all means, if you find something more suitable for us...' Dan gives me a sideway glance. I continue to eat.

'That's settled then,' Harry concludes.

We take our leave, and our heads are full of thoughts and questions.

'Are you unhappy here?' I ask after I put Nicky to bed.

'No, I am happy to be free. But you know that my ultimate goal is to live in England. My early childhood left the strongest impression. It marked me. You know all that. That is all we talked about and made plans for the future back in Bucharest. If there is an opportunity, why not take it?'

'But we have only just arrived. We are just beginning to settle. Nicky is happy; she has made so many friends. She is unsettled at school but given time she will settle down. I feel I owe it to this country, which has given us so much help, to repay some of that by working here.'

'We'll see how things go. Let's wait till Harry returns. We'll see what he has to say. In the meantime, nothing has changed,' Dan replies, and with that the conversation is over.

Harry leaves in the autumn after the High Holidays, and we spend most of the time at Sanda's after work and whenever we are free. Her house is always full of friends and laughter, and most important of all, Nicky is happy. I return late from work and find Nicky settled, fed and clean, and Sanda is supervising her homework - not that she or Dan could check if the work is done, because their Hebrew is most rudimentary. Most often Dan arrives before me and is comfortably seated and reading the English newspapers. Together, we go for a walk. On occasions we go to Jerusalem because Sanda loves shopping, looking for bargains in the small shops of the old town. Dan loves to haggle with the Arab shopkeepers and when they finally agree on a price, coffee on a copper tray is brought by a little boy. The coffee is served in minute cups and is bittersweet and refreshing. On our way back we stop at Hebron to buy fresh oranges from an old Arab man and exchange a few words with him. Dan drives our new Fiat car. He is very proud of it. He drives it recklessly with the 'macho' bravado of a youth.

Sanda and I are holding on to our seats petrified, while Nicky is often sick. Armed with plastic bags and paper towels, we drive on.

Work is increasingly demanding but I love it. Soon I acquire a few private patients. Once a month I also visit a place outside Beersheba to work with Bedouin women. They come accompanied by their husband or father, but never on their own. The men respectfully wait outside. There are lots of TB cases and implementing a programme of vaccination is hard work. Everything has to go for the Imam's approval, who will then advise the men to allow their wives or children to be vaccinated. It is said that the Imam has about 16 wives, many as young as his daughters. Some say that he meets the young women in the evening by the well and chooses a wife. I am not sure whether this is true. All I know is that men walk in front of women; they are the ones talking while the women stay shyly behind with their head down, rarely uttering a word.

Dan seems to be settled at the factory in Yerucham; he makes friends with his fellows workers, who are mostly from India and speak English. He plays checkers with the mayor and poker with our friends on a Friday evening. We take turns in hosting the parties. On occasions we travel to Tel Aviv or Haifa to visit the family. We take part in family events: Amnon's wedding to Shula, and the birth of Emmanuel and Lyorah's second child. I should be happy, and I think I am reasonably happy.

21
THE WIND CHANGES

Harry is back. It is spring, the beginning of a new decade, and he brings news. Life is good and he enjoyed his stay in West Germany; he has made friends and the company he works for is extending its business. That company has bought out an existing factory in the south of France, near Marseille, and has asked Harry to take over the running of it. Harry said that he knew another man who would like to come and work with him, and the invitation to work in the south of France extends to Dan, as Harry requested. There is a well-paid job waiting for Dan, and Harry is full of enthusiasm. He has it all planned: we should, all four of us, leave. The company will find us places to rent; there is no problem. We say nothing - too many things to think about.

At home we sit down and start talking. The mood is sombre, the air tense. I am totally against the project, as I don't want to plunge again into the unknown. It is all very well, but nobody seems to think that I have a profession, that I have my dreams too - it's not just about money. I would like to continue where I am. Sanda is a housewife and she can easily follow her man. They do not have children and broke all ties with their families long ago. They do not seem tinged with loyalty to anybody. But for me, things are different. Besides, what will I tell my family, who supported me all this time? I dread meeting them. I sense that Dan would like us to go. Loyalty is not high on his agenda either. I am worried: Nicky is registered on his passport and he would never contemplate parting from her. And I could not go through separation again. Oh dear, just when I thought we were settling and getting on better! We talk late into the night. It is clear to me that Dan wants to leave but, as usual, he expects me to say the word 'go' so that he will not carry any guilt or responsibility. I recognise this feature of his character well.

'Go if you want to! By yourself. Three or six months, maybe longer, whatever it takes. See if life there is as good as Harry says. If it is worth leaving everything behind and start again.'

'That is what I thought,' he says and I see that his face lights up, relieved from the burden of being the first to admit that this was what he wanted from the beginning. He did not have to make the decision. It is I who saw sense and will carry the responsibility.

He waits for us to switch off the light and go to bed. He wants to make love to me but I am not in the mood. I spend the remainder of the night thinking.

I can see some sense in what we've discussed: Dimona has nothing to offer in the long run. If we are to make progress, we will have to move to Tel Aviv, Haifa, Jerusalem or Beersheba. People do not stay long in Dimona. Nicky will grow up among her peers, become an Israeli, lose all her ties with her grandparents and the rest of the family, and join the Army - yet she will be different. She may have to take sides. Religion will become an issue. She already comes home from school and tells us that in her Religious Education class her teacher said that our God is the only true one, the only one worth fighting for. That other people, with their statues and paintings, believe in glorified dolls and fetishes. That makes both Dan and me very angry.

After Passover and Easter 1971 Dan is all set to go. He will leave with Harry and Sanda. Nicky and I move into their house to house-sit and dog-sit. It is more spacious, there is air conditioning, and it is nearer my office and Nicky's school. There is a garden and Nicky adores the dogs. We rent out our apartment to a family of newcomers.

Dan writes at least once a week. He has rented rooms in Valence. He describes it as a little town, quiet and opulent, very royalist in outlook and mentality. What he means is that people are formal and polite; there is no rubbish on the streets and life moves under precise rules. He takes his meals with Sanda and Harry. Sanda is a very good cook. At the weekends they explore the region. Sanda does not like the quaint villages much. She prefers Marseille or Lyon: she likes shopping.

Work at the factory on the Rhone Valley, near Valence, is interesting and well rewarded. He is the mechanical maintenance manager. His colleagues are pleasant; they eat lunch together in the canteen or in restaurants, but so far no one has invited him or Harry into their homes. Sanda made an effort and invited the neighbours from her building for morning coffee. Only a few replied and they never invited her back. Only one woman, a native of Morocco, appears friendlier. She tells Sanda that she moved in that building 25 years ago and is still considered a stranger.

The local Rabbi, having heard that there were Israelis in his town, comes to greet them. He invites the three Israelis to visit the synagogue. Little does he know that out of the three only one is Jewish. Dan insists that during the summer Nicky and I take a holiday and come to visit. It will be our first visit to France. I certainly would like a break and Nicky misses him. But in my mind, from time to time, I stop to think and wonder if I want to be with him. Is this is the opportunity that life has offered us again to part company? Yet there is an invisible tie that keeps us together.

We spend two weeks in France, where the climate is moderate. The town of Valence stands aloof and elegant among tropical trees and exotic foliage. The elegant villas stand away from the pavements but near enough to be visible. It is also a town of walls: high stone or brick walls with small gates, as if designed for secrets. Life pulsates behind those gates in inner courtyards away from the prying eyes of strangers. For the passer-by, the eerie quiet chills the bones. Nothing happens here, unlike the hustle and bustle of life that is quite overwhelming in Israel. Dan has rooms in such a house: a stone-built property on two floors hidden behind a stone wall as high as the building. The landlady - tall and bony, her skin tight over her angular unsmiling face - is lacking laughter lines. She must be in her fifties. We go for walks, Nicky and I, while Dan is out to work. Nicky skips along in front of me. 'Mammy, look, this lady! What a lovely dog!' She stretches her hand to pat the dog's head. The woman pulls the dog away abruptly, looking quite offended. 'Nicky,' I say, 'not everyone likes to have their dog touched. In future you have to ask for permission.'

We go to a playground and I smile at the children. The mothers give me a suspicious look and gather their offspring with a protective hand.

Harry and Sanda live in a new-ish apartment in a block of flats. The neighbours we meet on the stairs greet us with: '*Bonjour Madame.*' Sanda stops and introduces me. 'Hello,' I say with an open smile, 'my name is Miriam. It is nice to meet you.'

They give me a limp handshake and mumble their name: 'Madame Jobert' or 'Madame Pattou'. Without a further word, they turn and go away.

The second week Harry invites us for an excursion over the mountains to Aix-les-Bains, which is near the Swiss border. We drive north through meadows and valleys, mountains, forests, and acres and acres of golden wheat. The landscape, the villages and the auberges are beautiful, a testament to long traditions and love of the land. We arrive at Aix-les-Bains, situated on the lake Annecy, and I remember the verses of Lamartine:

One evening we two roamed - recall? - in silence
On waves and under heaven, far and wide,
No sound came save the cadence of the oarsmen
Stroking your tuneful tides
Suspend your trek o time! Suspend your flight
O favoring hours, and stay!
Let us pause, savouring the quick delight
That fills the dearest day.

The sheer delight of this wonderful place is marred by thoughts that are gathering in my head like storm clouds. I would like to go home, to put down roots. At the place that I now call home, in Dimona, I have most of the things that I want: work that I love, my child and a comfortable life. I have my freedom to travel wherever I want, whenever I want.

I know that Israel is a country at war, and sooner or later we will have to join in, one way or another, as there is no end in sight. I know that the general philosophy of the country, like any country at war, is very self-centred and ultra-nationalistic. I also know that Nicky needs her father; she has lost her grandparents and now her father is away. Her behaviour has deteriorated since he left. To everything I ask of her she replies: 'I don't want to!' her brow frowning and both shoulders moving up and down repeatedly in a gesture of rejection. She has lots of friends and would like to spend all the time outside playing. I would like her to sit down sometimes and do her homework or read a book. The problem is that I have so little time for family life: I have nothing much to offer outside the school to make her more interested, more eager to discover things. I don't drive so I can't take her to the sea. We could go by train on Saturday but trains and buses stop running from Friday evening till Saturday night. There are no films or performances to which I could take her. I cannot supervise her reading, since my own reading is not much good. I don't know... There is uneasiness in my universe. I am hoping, always hoping, that some event will turn up – something that will show me the road forward. I wonder if any day now Dan will write to me and say that he has decided to leave us and never come back. Perhaps that would be for the best.

But this does not happen. The tie is strong and still holds fast.

Just before Christmas, Dan is back. So are Sanda and Harry. They have made their decision and have come back to sell their house and move permanently to France.

Dan is not saying this: instead, he tells me what he has done. 'Just for information, you know, to have all the facts when we make a decision.'

He went to London and got information from the General Medical Council about my possible rights of practice in the UK. He also gathered information in France. He contacted old schoolmates and investigated the prospects of his employment in the UK.I have to pause and decide. *At last the chapter has turned to attention and the hush is beginning to stretch and you have to decide if you are a singer, a magician or a clown.* The lines of Sam Thompson from his book *Communion town* dance in my mind.

It is obvious that he wants us to go and has returned well-prepared, with enough ammunition to convince me. We can make a new beginning there. Yes, it is a special moment. 'I am hanging on your words,' he says.

At the end of four long weeks I give in. Time to go.

22
NEW YEAR 1972

'Let her be! She's just managed to fall asleep. The sea voyage is not for her. She is not a good traveller, poor child.'

'Anyway, we are here – the white cliffs, can you see?'

'Yes, I can see, but I have such a toothache; you must forgive me for not enjoying the view. When we are on dry land, if I find the strength, I will pick up a pebble and put it in my mouth. You do that when you set foot in a place where you've never been before, don't you? The old Romanian tradition.'

'Take a mouthful of whisky instead, and rinse. That will make you feel better. It won't be long, only about an hour to London.'

'It's so dark.'

'Well, wet and dark. That's not unusual here. It is winter after all. Keep your head right back so I can see both mirrors.'

A long silence follows. He has to concentrate on driving on the wrong side of the road, with the steering wheel on the left as well. The Fiat's engine is purring gently. I am trying to sleep but the tooth won't let me.

Indistinct homes and lots of foliage on ghostly trees whizz by, erasing the road markings in the dim light. Christmas already and not a patch of silvery white. Nicky is fast asleep on my lap. I must have dozed off. When I open my eyes, the purr of the engine has stopped.

A leafy, wide street immersed in the darkness on one side and shimmering white on the other revealing large, imposing houses comes into focus.

'Queen's Gate Hotel' says the yellow lit-up letters above the door. 'Wake up, Nicky, we've arrived!'

Dan says nothing but his eyes shine with contentment. It is an emotional time for him, and he greets London like a long-lost treasured relative. He busies himself with the luggage. I hold Nicky's hand and climb the steps. A tall man dressed in black and with a tall hat on his head ushers us in. The thought that perhaps Dickens is still alive crosses my mind – if not him then some of his Christmas characters. He is the concierge, and he takes our luggage and directs us to the reception. Inside it is all dark velvet and plush, with a hint of mothballs. The light from the wall lights is yellow. Large porcelain and china pots, and silver candlesticks stand sedately on well-polished dark chests and display cabinets. A few people are seated on deep, comfortable leather and velvet club chairs, arranged as near as possible to the fireplace. A friendly glow comes from the fire. This is definitely a Christmas setting, a once-upon-a-time. Pity I cannot enjoy it: I am tired and my tooth is persecuting me. Nicky is half-asleep, so we go to our room. Dan is busy filling forms, showing passports and directing the luggage.

Welcome to England! I climb the steps of the large stairway flanked by polished oak banisters. Last time I rode down on one of those, I must have been Nicky's age, or a little older, at our school. I don't know why I thought of that. A red runner is laid on the stairs, covering only the middle of each step.

'Mammy, do I walk on the carpet or on the wood?' Nicky pipes up, more awake now. The room has a double bed and a washbasin in a corner with separate taps: one for cold water and one for hot.

'Careful, Nicky, don't scald yourself,' Dan says. 'Put the plug in, fill the basin with half cold and half hot water, and then wash your hands and face.'

'Is that a towel?' I ask, holding a square of towelling material, no bigger than a small handkerchief.

'No, this is a flannel,' Dan says. 'It is for rubbing your face clean.' OK, first lesson's over. There is a bathtub and a toilet in a little enclosure attached to the room, but not a shower. We wash, get changed and go down to dinner.

The large dining room is lit by numerous pairs of wall lamps with little shades that throw a yellow light on several tables covered with white tablecloths and an array of china and silver-looking cutlery. It is New Year's Eve but still early. Just a few tables are occupied; two elderly ladies dressed in black, their silver hair turned gold by the light, smile at Nicky. 'What a fair child,' one says. Another table is occupied by a solitary elderly man dressed in a black tuxedo and a white shirt. It is all so quiet.

'Where is the music?' I ask, my head full of memories of other New Year's Eve nights. How we used to have them in Bucharest to greet the New Year!

'Oh, we English do not celebrate the New Year,' says the waiter with a dismissive smile, when Dan asks. 'That is more of a Scottish habit.'

Dinner comes: meat, two kinds of potatoes - some roasted, some boiled - and some boiled cabbage. We are hungry, and I add salt to everything to make it palatable.

'Where is the bread?' Nicky asks

'Yes, I could do with some,' Dan replies. 'Waiter!'

The man approaches and his eyes grow wide with surprise. 'Bread, Sir? I will see what I can find.'

He returns with some dry rolls and some butter that we didn't ask for.

'I forgot that they don't serve bread with dinner - not like us Romanians, bread with everything.'

That is how it is going to be from now on: lesson after lesson.

It is the New Year 1972. We wake up to a new day and a new year but my tooth gives me the same trouble that it gave me last year. We ask the receptionist to put us in touch with an emergency dental service. However, for every number they ring, the same question is asked: are you registered with a dentist? Who is your dentist? No. We are not registered: we arrived yesterday. Is there a place where visitors can get emergency help? There is the Leicester Dental Hospital but it is closed for the holiday. I'll manage: I have no choice. The next day is the same and finally, on the third day, we go to that hospital. The tooth is beyond salvation so it comes out and I am given antibiotics. I am so happy and relieved! After a couple of hours' rest, I join my two and we go for a walk. It is the first time I actually notice what is around me. What a strange magical town! All black, white, red and green! The large expanse of green of the parks and the black imposing buildings washed down by torrents of sooty rainwater, which has created its own lacy patterns but has never succeeded in washing down the coal soot. Dan is our guide. Excitement fills his voice and eyes: I have not seen him so animated since his arrival in the free world.

Big Ben, Westminster, Whitehall, the tall gothic churches, Trafalgar Square, Piccadilly, Peter Pan's statue and the double-decker red buses which are Nicky's delight - again, I feel I have stepped into a different, enchanted world.

23
DAN'S LONDON

Dan is in his element. He loves showing us the city he dreamt about for so many dark years when stuck in Romania. I see in his eyes and the way he moves that he 'owns' this city. For him this is the promised land. He takes us to Kensington Park, where grown men fly kites and sail little boats on the lake, just like they did when Dan was a child, in spite of the raging war. On High Street Kensington he shows us the big stores: Barkers where he used to go shopping with his mother and sister; his mother asked his opinion about new dresses she was trying on. But the house where he lived has gone, demolished, to make room for the new, large motorway. He shows Nicky his first school: the vicarage of St Mary's C of E school for girls is still here.

'Only the girls' school was left,' he tells us, 'so I went to a girls' school. My name was Victor Pickard then: we were told to change our names.'

'Did you have friends to play with?' Nicky asks wistfully.

'Yes, I had two good friends. One was from Bulgaria and the other from Poland. I remember their names but they might not have been their real ones either.'

He tells Nicky childhood stories that I have never heard before: how his mother took him on short holidays to Box Hill and a proper holiday one summer to Weston-Super-Mare, and how he checked the mailbox every morning for letters from his father. In his room he had a map on the wall with little flags and he marked each time his father's location, as it was explained in his father's letters. He also marked the position of the front. Nicky listens, her eyes wide and her mouth slightly open, and urges him to tell more.

He remembers one morning when he was sent by his mother to buy milk and the daily newspaper, and on the way back the sirens started sounding their warning sound of approaching bombardment. He heard the doodlebug approaching and then silence, and then a hiss and he just about managed to reach the Underground station when the explosion happened. He explains to Nicky what a doodlebug is. When it was over, he went home and found his mother crying, holding his sister tight.

'Why did she cry? Wasn't she happy to see you?' Nicky asks.

'Because she did not know what had happened to me or how to find me.'

We return to the hotel, all thinking our own thoughts.

'Daddy, do you think the Queen will invite us to tea?'

'Perhaps,' he says, 'but only if she is at home. See? There is no flag flying on the roof of the palace. It means she is not in.'

24
THE GENERAL MEDICAL COUNCIL

'What an ugly building, not very inviting. All concrete and brick stained by the traffic. I have this feeling that it does not hold any promise for me.'

'It was built in a hurry after the war, large enough to shelter all the administrators,' Dan replies. 'It is because of this noisy and polluted roundabout. The place was bombed to ruins during the war. They had to rebuild - and fast!'

'Perhaps the enemy didn't like the name? Elephant and Castle!'

Dan hastens to explain that once there was a pub with that name on that place, although the popular belief is that it was where the Infanta de Castilla was housed during her stay in England. Whatever the truth, only the name survives. It now houses the GMC: the General Medical Council - the 'white elephant'.

We are directed to take a little number from a tiny machine, and advised to sit and wait for the number to be called. The room is almost full: it is hard to find a chair. I am sitting next to Dan and, on my left, a young man starts talking to me. Seeing that I am unresponsive, he starts speaking Italian. I let him speak and from the little Italian I understand, he is saying that he is a doctor, born in Greece, who studied medicine in Italy. An Italian doctor can practise freely in the UK, but a Greek one can't. Although he studied in Italy and has an Italian degree, he was refused registration because of his nationality. He is here to appeal. I look at Dan, a question mark forming in my eyebrows. What is going on? He is busy talking to another man on his right, an Asian-looking gent with curly hair. When they stop their conversation, Dan turns to me and tells me in Romanian what he heard.

'This doctor is from Pakistan: he graduated some years ago from the University of Lahore. After graduation, most of his colleagues came to the UK and they were automatically received to practise as fully qualified doctors. This man chose to stay behind and work a few years in his hometown. He got married and then applied to come to England. But this year Pakistan came out of the Commonwealth and, because of that, full registration rights were withdrawn. He has to pass further exams under supervision in order to qualify. Rather strange,' Dan says.

Strange indeed: with the same qualifications from the same school, one can be recognised as a doctor and another refused, depending on political events and government's decisions in one's country. It's not about medicine: it's about politics.

I am glad that I have not officially resigned from my position in Dimona; I just took three months' unpaid leave. Perhaps we could go back?

My number is called. Dan moves forward and starts speaking on my behalf. I can practise as a junior doctor in hospitals, we are told. After three years I can sit an examination and obtain an English degree LRCP MRCS. We fill in forms and submit copies of my documents, and the clerk behind the window reassures us that I will receive an answer in about five to six months. If my application is accepted, I will be sent to work under supervision in a teaching hospital for a one-month assessment. I feel better because this at least gives me a respite to go and learn the language.

We return to the hotel and Dan goes out to find accommodation. He will have to return in a few more days to France and his work. Nicky and I will have to move on our own. That will be fun! A bitter smile curls on my lips.

25
ON THE MOVE

It is a Tuesday, a week into the new year, and time to move. Dan has found an apartment, arranged for the transport of our belongings, said 'Goodbye, see you in a fortnight,' and left. We agreed that we could not afford for him to lose his job. Before he left, he wrote to a friend of his father, now a lord with a residence in Eaton Square, in the hope that he will see him on his return and get some advice.

As for me? I am again, as I had been in Italy, somewhere I have never been before, unable to speak the language. I am more experienced now, I tell myself: I managed then and I will manage now. The difference is that now I also have the responsibility of my child, and I care that she does not feel again displaced and unsettled.

The doorman with the top hat hails a taxi, and we leave the elegant sedate Kensington Queen's Gate and travel west. It is a cold and humid grey day. Silver white like a frozen blanket covers the large expanse of green of Clapham Common and Putney. Here and there, a patch of green pushes through and does not give up the fight. Come spring, it will emerge again.

Streatham, Clapham, Putney, Wimbledon… They must have been villages once: houses and churches, and markets and schools grouped around the commons. As they grew in size, they spread, joined up with London and became Greater London. We head for SW19.

'See, Mammy, there are children playing.' Nicky is all eyes, eager to discover new sights. I sense that she can't wait to find some children and go out to play.

Here we are: we have arrived in Wimbledon, our destination. We pass through a shopping centre, with shops much smaller than in Central London; a large supermarket, Sainsbury's, dominates the commercial street. The road turns left, climbing slightly, and as we advance, the street becomes larger and the houses more cared for. The pavement is shaded by trees that have lost their leaves to winter. We turn right. Edge Hill is a street with elegant detached Victorian villas surrounded by large gardens and foliage, and at its pinnacle there is the imposing Catholic church with its tall steeple. At the end of the road is the back of the tennis courts. We stop at number 12. A woman in her late forties comes to greet us; she is very tall, with a beautiful oval-shaped face, large sparkling eyes and an engaging smile. I cannot help noticing her large hips out of which emerge a pair of sturdy legs. She towers over me. Her black hair is plaited on each side of her head and the plaits are knotted together on top of her head in a fashion long gone. She greets us in

English but I detect a strong sing-song accent, somehow familiar; I have heard it before. I learn soon that she is Hungarian. She speaks German but not French, and my German is rusty. At least I understand it better than English. Our rooms are large and airy, and the floors are covered in a wall-to-wall grey carpet. There is a bedroom, a sitting room and dining room. There is a smallish kitchen and a bathroom. I am satisfied; Dan has chosen well. I start unpacking while Nicky goes out to inspect the premises.

Soon she returns with information: 'Mammy, the lady's name is Priscilla and the old man is her husband. You should see his whiskers! He is called Victor, and he is an architect and a writer.'

'How on earth did you find this out?'

Nicky shrugs her shoulders, Israeli fashion. 'She told me. She also said I have to be quiet because Victor does not like children.'

I stand dumbfounded, trying to figure out how she understood all this. Well, if this is true, it is not good news. However, Nicky will soon be in school, if I can find one; she won't be around much during the day. We go out in the early afternoon to buy some food. Closing time is 5 o'clock and I've been warned; nothing will be open after that. It is a fair distance to the shops and it gives us a chance to look at the buildings, the gardens and the people passing by. I am wondering who lives in those large imposing houses. Are they large families or are all those properties divided into flats like the one we just leased? What do people do for a living to be able to afford those houses? Some gardens are well tended, while others have been left to grow wild. Priscilla and Victor Hattar's garden is one of the latter: paved in the middle, the rest is left to nature. A very old maroon Rolls-Royce languishes at the side of the wall, weeds threatening to engulf it. We walk to Sainsbury's before it closes. It is the first time I go shopping in the UK; it takes a while to negotiate the pounds and pints, and work out their values in grams and litres. It does not take long for me to realise that meat is much cheaper than in Israel but vegetables… That's different. It is OK for onions, potatoes and carrots but when it comes to peppers, aubergines, tomatoes, garlic, lettuce and fresh herbs, it is a different story. They are sold as single items at an exorbitant price – if they are there at all. Fruit is apples and pears. Lots of products that I am used to buying are not on the shelves. I wonder at corned beef, potted beef, piccalilli and chutney. I have never heard of them and I am not prepared to try. I'll wait for Dan. I just get the basics: meat and potatoes, bread, eggs and milk. And a square white loaf, already sliced! At the till the cashier asks me for something and five shillings. I have no idea what she wants, so I open my purse and invite her to take whatever she needs. She does it with a smile, explaining each coin and note in the change. Then she says, 'Thank you,' when I should be the one thanking her.

26
AT THE HATTARS'

Priscilla, the landlady, shows us around our new lodgings, which once belonged to Victor's mother. She speaks German slowly, like a schoolgirl, her Hungarian inflection strong. That makes it easier for me to understand. She explains the rules, repeating on several occasions that they don't normally accept families with children and that Nicky's presence must not interfere in any way with her husband's writing. Nicky must never approach his study, make a noise, or play on the communal stairway or landings. I am a little scared by this reception and begin to dread meeting Victor. However, when we finally do meet, he is polite and even pleasant.

It is Priscilla's idea to have a party in our honour. She wants to help me find a school for Nicky and understands my difficulties. I feel this is very generous of her. Her plan is to invite neighbours who have children of Nicky's age and who can advise me. Indeed, the following Saturday the next-door neighbours with their four children and another lady from further down the road with her two come to tea. All of a sudden, the large room fills up with words, laughter and children's shrieks, and I feel deaf, dumb and lost. Priscilla takes me by the hand and introduces me to another woman, whom I have not previously noticed.

'This is my friend Ursula,' she says. 'We worked in the same office for a while. She speaks French and German.'

'*Bonjour*, are you French?' I ask.

'No,' she replies, 'I am from Switzerland.'

'Have you lived here long?'

'I came here when I was 18 as an au pair to learn English and stayed on.'

She kindly offers to translate for me. I smile at this pale woman. She must be my age, and her eyes acknowledge my relief at her being there. She has a soft voice and when she speaks, she bends her head to make eye contact as if to reassure me. Later on, as our friendship grew, I learned from her lots of things about people around me.

The party is a great success. Priscilla is beaming with happiness. I will later find out that she had been trying for ages to invite her neighbours into her home. They are well-established English families of higher social standing, some even titled. Priscilla wanted to be accepted and make friends, and this occasion proves to be a good opportunity. She is thrilled that the countess, who lives next door, agrees willingly to help me, a new immigrant, to place my daughter in school. Priscilla serves freshly made scones with cream and butter, and home-made jam, and she offers tea with milk, in fine china cups. The guests congratulate her and spend some time discussing the merits of different tea labels. I drink my tea without milk; I will try it later with milk and see if I like it. In the meantime, I make a great effort to catch, here and there, a word that I understand. Soon my head is spinning and I become listless. I watch my daughter with a mixture of pride and envy. How quickly she begins to play with the other children present, communicating in a language without words.

Soon the talk turns to schools. Ursula keeps translating: state schools which are not public and church schools of various denominations, some public and some fee-paying. It is all too much. I come from a system of state education, free for all. I stop listening. Instead, I watch the friendly faces of the guests and think that this is a most welcoming party to my new country. Pity that Dan is missing it. I think of impressions I had formed from books saying that the English are a cold race and that their homes are their castles, with impenetrable walls.

Myths begin to be dispelled.

27
THE LANDLORD

Victor arrived in England while the Hungarian uprising was raging in 1956. He took with him his secretary - his secret lover - and his old mother, and crossed the border into the free world. He came to England where he had a few friends and a few followers. He is a writer of philosophy, essays and anti-communist pamphlets. He was hated by the Hungarian Government because he was a dissident. Victor is also a trained architect. He is at least 20 years older than Priscilla. She is very attractive and inspires confidence, coming across as a woman who can do anything. She adores Victor and takes great care of all his needs. He loves to be adored and revered. He pays much attention to his appearance, intent on creating an almost theatrical image of a true Gabor, the romantic Hungarian gipsy. He wears a black hat with a large brim over his shoulder-length silvery hair. Large white moustaches twisted upwards at the ends adorn his cheeks, giving the large head an image of power and hidden passion. He is very strict: his word is law and Priscilla is only too happy to cater for all his desires. A few months after their arrival, she found a job as an assistant accountant, where language fluency - or the lack of it - was not a major problem, as she was employed to record numbers in ledgers.

She spends the weekends cleaning and cooking enough dishes for the whole week, making sure that they are varied and tasty. Then she divides the food into individual portions so that Victor will only have to warm it up and eat. She uses the hoover for cleaning only when Victor allows it. When he is writing, Victor demands complete silence; nobody is allowed to enter his room and the telephone is disconnected.

Victor has a practical side as well. Soon after their arrival in the UK, with money from his friends, he bought a derelict Victorian villa on Edge Hill, an imposing property which he set about restoring. He made the first floor comfortable for his mother and he reserved the ground floor for himself and Priscilla. He rented out the top-floor rooms, which once belonged to the servants, as self-contained studios. In time he became more devoted to Priscilla and more dependent on her. He gradually distanced himself from his mother. He married Priscilla late, after his arrival in the UK, having previously shared all his life with his mother. It was Mama and he during the war, during his schooling and during the hard times under communists. The elderly woman was sad and hated Priscilla, who completely took over all duties from her. Victor's life in the meantime remained the same as it always was. Replacing one woman with the other was barely perceptible to him. He continued to be adored. His mother blamed

Priscilla and even more so when Victor, at Priscilla's persistent demands, made all the arrangements to bring her daughter over from Budapest. Priscilla had been a married woman when she left Hungary to be with Victor and she had left her only daughter behind. Soon after her arrival, the 17-year-old daughter proved to be a nuisance for Victor, diverting her mother's attention away from him. Victor's mother hated both women and cursed the day she had come to England. One day, they found her dead. Mama had taken a full bottle of her heart pills. Victor was distraught and aggrieved. He blamed Priscilla's daughter. He bought for himself, perhaps as a comforter, a 1930s Rolls-Royce at an auction. It needed a lot of work to be able to function and although he spent a lot of his time sitting in it, he did not have the mechanical knowledge to restore it to life. So it remained abandoned in the garden, covered in weeds. But it served its purpose: Victor could sit on the luxurious leather car seats and meditate. The situation in the household became so unpleasant that the young daughter had to leave. She found a position as an au pair in Rome and peace was restored in the household in Edge Hill.

28
WE GO TO SCHOOL

The following Monday, Ursula returns and offers to speak to the Local Education Authority on my behalf, conveying to them my request that Nicky go to a non-denominational state school near where we live, a school which receives non-English-speaking children. Within two weeks we get a place. It is Peppy's School. Nicky will have English classes in the morning and join in the other school activities in the afternoon. It is a C of E school, with a good reputation and within walking distance. It is the only one available, so I accept. The children are nice and soon she makes friends. The school has a strong music department and I rent a cello for her from the department. It is Nicky's choice and I am thrilled that she is beginning to take an interest in something other than play. In Dimona I was getting quite concerned about her lack of willingness to learn and the fact that she often ran away from school.

I am amazed at the speed at which she makes progress with the language - much faster than I do. I study eight to ten hours a day, learning words one by one, while she comes out with full sentences without worrying what each word means. She is not translating; she is just talking.

It soon becomes obvious to me that my progress with spoken language is much too slow, although my understanding is improving. It is time to get some help. I join an adult class in English as a second language at Merton College in Morden, on Priscilla's advice. The class is small: two middle-aged Asian ladies, a Turkish couple from Cyprus, a Portuguese man of uncertain age and a Chinese lady. The Asian ladies bring their knitting with them and speak almost continually in their native language; the Turkish man has to repeat the same word to his wife several times for her to understand. By the third lesson, I reach the point of despair. It is all too slow. The young teacher looks lost and the homework, which I do without fail, has to be repeated, as only two or three of us present complete it on time for the next lesson. At this rate, it will take me years to master enough language to enable me to work. I don't have years to waste. We need money; we need a home.

Dan comes the following weekend. He is a little disappointed that he has not received any replies to his applications for work. Dan is earning well in France, but this is not what he and I want. He proposes that I try the Berlitz language school. It was famous when his mother went there and it is still. The difficulty is that the school is in Central London, on Oxford Street. It means that Nicky will have to come home from school by herself in the afternoon at least three times a week. In Israel that was no problem - children as young as three took themselves to nursery - but here most parents bring and collect their children. Nicky is quite happy to come home from school by herself in the company of a few older girls who live nearby. I give her the key and I beg her to be quiet and never disturb Victor.

One day the train is late coming home. As I open the entrance door, I hear voices. Victor's study door is open and as I pass by, I look in and my heart misses a beat. Nicky is standing, looking over Victor's shoulder, while he draws a bird perched on a tree branch. When he has finished, he gives it to Nicky. I begin to apologise, stumbling on my words but he interrupts me, saying that they had a lovely time and that he welcomed the break.

There is a fair distance from Edge Hill to the station. I walk along the street at least three afternoons a week and on the way I look at the massive well-kept villas. I dream that one day perhaps we will have one - maybe not so grand but nice and cosy, and with a lovely garden and a dog. The journey from Wimbledon to Oxford Street is full of new adventures and discoveries. First of all, I learn never to rely on timetables. The trains are almost always late. The platforms announced on the board can change at the last minute and I cannot understand the announconcretes; the loudspeakers are too loud and the sounds are distorted. Besides, the speech comes in all sorts of strange accents. It is much easier to ask someone or follow the crowd. At Wimbledon it is easy to find a seat because it is the end of the line, but coming back from Oxford Street is different. I learn what rush hour is. I marvel at how people can read their newspapers unperturbed, standing up, squashed up and balancing on each other.

On the way back I do my shopping. I learn that a pound in weight is half a kilo - but not quite - that a shilling used to be 12 old pennies but is now 5p and that a pint is more than half a litre. I learn to say 'please' and 'thank you' for everything. And if someone asks a question or an address or which bus to take and I do not know the answer, I have to say I feel sorry, as if it were my fault. At home I learn that tea must be brewed for three minutes precisely after warming the pot and served with milk. There is controversy over whether one pours milk before or after the tea. And the jury is still out. I learn my lesson not to buy turkey or chicken because after cooking the meat tastes of fish. That is because poultry is fed with fish flour feed till the birds are slaughtered.

I call the post 'Royal Mail' because that is what is written on the vans and the people laugh out loud. 'It may be Royal but we call it just the post or the mail,' they say.

People are nice and helpful, without crowding me or asking too many questions. In the evening I keep the television on most of the time in the hope that I will understand a little more of what is being said. I watch *Coronation Street* because it is easier to follow; Mrs Walker and Deidre become my friends. *EastEnders* is too difficult. I watch *Old Grey Whistle Test* and the charts. I've missed out on the Beatles and the Rolling Stones in Romania; I have to make up for lost time. I can't wait for *Top of the Pops*. I even start reading the Agatha Christie books that I have read before in translation, and Mills and Boons. They are written in a language I can cope with. I listen faithfully to the news, and become acquainted with Enoch Powell and his 'rivers of blood'. He seems so passionate about immigration. I listen to the Irish problems but I don't understand what's going on.

At the language school I learn more words and sentences. The charming young teacher comes from Australia. I learn from her how the verbs change according to the preposition: put on, put off, put out and put through have entirely different meanings. I learn that Londoners finish every conversation with a question: 'isn't it?' – or, more accurately, 'innit?'

29
DAN IS LOOKING FOR WORK

Every fortnight Dan comes over. It is a long way from Valence to Wimbledon. He drives the Fiat and makes the journey in ten hours. I shudder to think of the speed and the risks he is taking. He looks exhausted but determined. He is anxious but tries to hide it from me and from Nicky. Together we scan the papers that I bought for him the previous Tuesday when the job section advertisements appear in the *Telegraph* and *The Times*. The adverts state clearly that foreign graduates will be considered only if the position is not filled by a British applicant. Dan says that his application form is invariably late; it is more than a week since it was first advertised, and on several occasions he is told on the telephone that the list is closed. The majority of good jobs will be considered only after they are offered to British people and vacancies are not filled. All the managerial positions state clearly that jobs will be available for overseas graduates only if no suitable candidate is selected.

So far no interview or reply. The waiting is killing us. We managed to get together, yet we are drifting apart. It seems that we have spent most of our life waiting: waiting to be allowed to leave, to be together, for me to start a life in the UK, for Dan to get a job and to settle finally into a normal family routine. We are not getting any younger. The news on television and papers reflects the country's mood. According to various speakers, the fear of the invasion is imminent. This time it's not the Germans or the Jews: it's the foreign workers, especially Asians and black people from the old colonies which are no more.

Dan perseveres; he does not complain. If he is anxious, he does not show it; he tries to hide it. We tour the country. We drive to Hampton Court, Kew Gardens, Brighton and, of course, Central London. He parks anywhere. He realised soon enough that with foreign number plates one gets a polite reminder rather than a fine.

We did not expect that it would be so hard for him to find employment and much easier for me. After all, it was he who lived in England before and speaks the language fluently. But it does not seem to count. The people he knew, friends of his father, are sympathetic but cannot help. In March I receive a letter from the GMC. I am advised that on 1 May I should present myself to the Royal London Hospital for one month's work under supervision. I will be assessed and the consultant in charge will advise the council if I am competent to work as a doctor in this country.

Panic begins to set in, mostly because my Berlitz class comes to an end. The teacher tells us that she is pregnant. She is single and she was advised to leave.

There is no immediate replaconcrete. I decide to go to the GMC to ask if they can recommend a suitable school. I stop someone at Embankment Underground station and ask how to get to Elephant and Castle.

'Sorry, love, I don't speak any foreign,' he says and hurries away. So much for my efforts! I get the map out and start walking. It is not that far. I am advised that there is a course for overseas medical graduates at Kennington College, which is just round the corner. That is what I need: perhaps it will help so I go and register. There I meet again the young Spanish doctor who was in my class at the Berlitz school. She is working as a nanny while waiting for GMC registration. We become friends. The two lady teachers are friendly and encourage us to speak. We learn that the patient may not complain of diarrhoea but would say that they have 'the runs'. The abdomen is the 'tummy' or the 'belly'. Anything gynaecological is 'the privates'; periods are 'the curse' or the 'monthlies'. I learn that urine is 'waterworks'. I also learn the difference in meaning between sore and painful. 'Montezuma's revenge' makes me laugh once I understand the meaning. I learn that people like to have a tonic in a bottle or something to rub on and that they don't much like injections, which they often call 'jabs'. I discover that the English never complain – they have a 'stiff upper lip'. 'A bun in the oven' means pregnancy. These expressions do not always make much sense to me and I especially struggle to understand why the patient will not take in what you say unless you repeat the word 'serious' several times during the conversation. The word 'actually' is used quite often. I learn that if one asks about family, they usually mean children - not sisters, brothers or parents. I learn that there are two kinds of 'funny'- funny peculiar and funny ha-ha - and to be careful how I pronounce or write the word 'sheath'.

When we are together at home, we are stressed, impatient and snappy with each other and with Nicky. When I am on my own, I wish he were here. The general mood, reflected in the papers and on television, is against foreign workers. Enoch Powell proposes to give black people £1,000 to go home. Go where after the life they made here for themselves?

On 1 May I present myself at the London Hospital, where I am told that it would be better for me to have my assessment at the London Jewish Hospital in Stepney Green, which is part of the same group. I wonder if this is because I come from Israel. They are expecting me, the secretary says, and my assessor will be Dr Gordon.

The London Jewish is a newer building which stands three floors high on an old, narrow street lined with dark, neglected, small Victorian houses in Stepney Green. I meet the hospital secretary who introduces me to Dr Gordon; he then takes me to visit the hospital and introduces me to the staff. It is a small hospital, which was once a charity hospital built by the Jewish community for the predominantly Jewish population of the East End. In time, the Jews moved on and out of the area to be replaced by a multi-ethnic population composed of Irish, Indian, Pakistani, Jews, Turkish and Greek immigrants, and native English people. The London Jewish was recently affiliated to the Royal London and serves the local population. There is an Internal Medicine department, as well as a surgical ward, a children's ward and a few beds reserved for Dermatology. The consultants, top London specialists, who in the past offered their services and expertise free of charge, are employed now that the hospital has become part of the Royal London. Dr Gordon is a small man with kind eyes. His silver hair shines in the light. He is the most senior member of the hospital: a physician and a well-known gastroenterologist who was one of the first to introduce gastric endoscopy in England. There is also a second consultant, a Dr Fassina. I shake hands with the consultants and the matron, who is a large woman dressed in a dark blue dress with a large silver clasp adorning her protruding abdomen. She wears dark stockings and black lace-up shoes. On her head is a white lace starched cap which stands almost suspended on top of her greying hair.

The wards are large rooms with a row of 24 beds, each set in pairs facing each other and separated by a large refectory table with chairs spread round. This is for the nurses to sit when they have a moment and doubles up as a dinner table at lunch. Green cotton curtains move on rails, separating a bed from the others. There are female wards and male wards joined by a middle hall. Each ward has a sister in charge on both sides, male and female. She wears a blue uniform and a belt with a silver buckle. Her coif is slightly smaller than the matron's and it is also white. I am introduced to Sister May, who is in charge of the medical wards, and Sister Delaney, who is in charge of the surgical wards. The children's ward has a Sister who is from Austria. There are staff nurses to help them; they wear blue-and-white striped uniforms and a silver buckle on their blue belt to show that they are fully qualified nurses. There are student nurses and also state registered nurses. I cannot yet make the distinction. The Austrian Sister speaks with a heavy German accent. The night sister speaks with a Jamaican accent.

The second medical consultant, Dr Fassina, is Canadian and he works as a long-term locum. I nod my head, signalling that I understand everything, although I understand nothing. I am introduced also to one of the visiting consultants, a very tall man with nervous hands and an abrupt manner. He is a cardiologist from King's College Hospital, apparently very famous. I also meet the paediatric consultant who comes once a week, a Dr Dickson; he is also a consultant to the Queen, and his wife is a dame. I'll ask Dan what being a dame means. I thought that it goes without saying that a woman is a dame – aren't all women dames?

30
ASSESSMENT

From the start I get into trouble with the Sisters. The Irish one is gentler, but the Austrian and the Scottish ones are very strict. The night sister is black and from Jamaica. She wears a wig with straight hair. I don't understand any of them if they speak quickly. When I go to visit the wards, I am told not to step inside the door without Sister's permission. This is strange. Where I come from, it is the doctor who gives nurses permission and tells them what to do, not the other way round.

One of my first impressions is how kind the staff are to the patients. They smile and speak quietly; they do not shout out orders. If a patient refuses something, they listen, go away and come back later, asking the patient if he or she is ready. The patients are allowed to smoke in the ward. They can choose to eat while in bed, but if they can walk, they are encouraged to go to the long table, which is transformed into a dinner table. The tea lady is black. She wears a pink-and-white uniform, and is jolly and chatty with the patients. I marvel at how kind and patient with the sick everyone is. The only sign of authority appears when the Sister directs the student nurses. They wear lighter blue dresses, and their headdress is simple and white. I hide a smirk when the Austrian Sister shouts at the student nurses: 'Chop, chop! Mouvy der arsh!'

I am invited to attend the clinics, where new patients referred by their family doctors are seen first by the consultant, and also where patients discharged from in-hospital care are followed up and seen by the registrar or the houseman, and continue to be monitored and advised. To me that's new and I think it is wonderful. The letters from the family doctors are friendly: sometimes they ask for advice, as they are not embarrassed to write that they don't know something. Dr Gordon says that sometimes he sees patients only to reassure them and their doctor, and that is enough.

'Two heads are better than one,' he says.

I notice that most local doctors address him by his first name - something I would never dare to do - as though they are long-standing personal friends. From time to time, Dr Gordon asks me to diagnose some complaint or to offer my thoughts on treatment. I do my best. Sometimes I stumble, but he is very patient. He even lets me assist him when he performs a stomach endoscopy on a patient, as this is a very new form of investigation and he is one of the first specialists to have introduced it to the UK. I sit in at the cardiology clinic. Dr Zoob is a man with a temper, who puts me down with every word I say, so I am frightened to say much. Some terms are confusing: in Romanian we say 'insufficiency' while in English the term is 'incompetence'. The meaning is the same - the aortic valves do not work well - but he refuses to try to understand. He yells at me, his nervous hands twitching, and I tremble with shame and a sense of failure. The registrar does not lose any time and spreads the word around. I am getting a little paranoid. I feel that everyone is looking down on me, but Dr Gordon, the paediatrician Dr Dickson and the dermatologist Dr Marr are very encouraging. Dr Fassina tends to explain everything without asking questions; he has a gift for teaching. I like his broad Canadian accent.

Every day I feel like a schoolgirl before an exam, with my tummy in knots and my heart beating rhythmically in my ears. There are lots of things I don't know, but I don't dare to ask in case it reflects on my ability. I would love someone to show me how the emergency trolley works; we never had one at my country hospital in Romania or in Dimona. I would like to be given a chance to practise how to use a plastic cannula and insert it in a vein. We only used needles and rubber tubing, and even those were handled only by the nurses. Every day I get headaches. At the end of the clinics, which usually run late, I rush out to catch the Tube and go back to Wimbledon. By that time Nicky has been back for at least two hours, and I am wondering what mischief she's been up to and what I will find on my return. However, she seems to manage well. She's learned how to make tea and toast, and I find her either playing with her friends outside or in front of the television. I am very tired and I have a splitting headache but I have to listen to Nicky. She has made a new friend; her name is Angela, and Angela's mother has sent a note inviting us to dinner. I hurry to cook our evening meal - nothing complicated, just grilled chops and potatoes. While this is cooking, I listen to the news. After the meal, Nicky practises her cello, which she enjoys doing, and I open my books to improve my English and brush up on my medical knowledge. As I consider what I have learned that day, the cello is screeching in the background.

The next day I walk Nicky to school. It is a little early, but I leave her in the lollipop lady's care and take the train from the nearby station, in a panic that I will be late. Once at the hospital, I put on my white coat and wait in the doctor's mess for the consultants to arrive and to accompany them on their ward round.

The mess is a lovely room with soft lounge chairs and coffee tables, a television set and a radio. A telephone set, connecting to all wards and the switchboard, hangs on the wall. A large counter separates the kitchen corner. There is a kettle, teapot, cutlery and a fridge. I am told that no outside food can be brought in, except for vegetables and fruit, and that there is an inspector of food, who I gather by the description is a Jewish *shomer*. When I meet him, this first impression is confirmed. He is wearing a black silk caftan which is stained with all the menus he has ever inspected. My old resentment against religious interference threatens to bubble to the surface.

I meet the junior doctors, resident staff. There is a senior surgical houseman who is from Lebanon and is studying to become a surgeon. He lives in one of the hospital rooms with his young, pretty wife. She spends most of her time in the doctor's mess, waiting for her husband. She is from Ramala, in Palestine. The surgical registrar is an elderly Bengali man and the medical registrar is Indian, and he has something to say about everyone - usually negative comments. He aspires to be a consultant and resents the long-term locum consultant, Dr Fassina. He thinks that he deserves to be a consultant himself. He also thinks that everyone is beneath him and rather stupid. I am surprised to find so many nationalities in a London Jewish hospital. But I am told that Dr Gordon is adamant that there should be no discrimination and that Jews should not do to others what was done to them in the past. However, Dr Sing, the registrar, thinks that there is discrimination against black people and Asians. I feel a little uncomfortable and slightly isolated - perhaps because I am older than most of them.

I join my colleagues for lunch. We get on reasonably well, although on a few occasions the atmosphere gets a little tense when images of violence and skirmishes between Palestinians and Israelis appear on television.

31
THE FIRST APPOINTMENT

The month of May goes very quickly: a whirlwind of tension, emotions and headaches.

'Well, how quickly the month has gone by. We thank you for joining us. I am happy to sign your certificate of competence,' Dr Gordon says and we shake hands.

'Thank you and everyone for your support,' I say but what I am thinking is: *What next? Where do I go from here? How do I start looking for a job?* There are only a few days left and then my assignment will be completed.

During the afternoon at the next outpatient clinic I meet Dr Fassina, who asks me to speak with him at the end of the session. I tell this to Dr Gordon who is aware of this request and encourages me to wait. It is getting late, well after 5 o'clock, and Dr Fassina has not seen the last patient yet. My mind is torn between staying on and going to meet Nicky, who by now will be back from school. I call Priscilla and explain, and she promises to look out for Nicky.

Dr Fassina is one of those men who fill a room or any space; he is tall and heavyset, and he has a booming voice. He is not young; he must be almost 60. His cheeks are criss-crossed by thin red veins. His manner is direct, and he makes a habit of speaking his mind and embarrassing people without quite offending them. He wears spectacles framed by dark square frames. When he wants to read something, he takes his glasses off and peers closely at the papers. I sit in the mess, scanning the BMJ and searching the advertisements for jobs while I wait. I have to telephone to ask for an application form and I am still fearful of the telephone. He finally appears and, without any introduction, says: 'My houseman is leaving in two weeks. Want his job? It's yours if you feel like it!'

I am taken aback. Contradictory thoughts start rushing round my head, one on top of the other, fighting for priority: Nicky, job, money, Dan, distances, security, Nicky and money again. My parents need help. Dan's parents need support. They are waiting for a visa to be able to come out. At their ages they will need help. So I say yes, I will consider his offer, and thank him.

'OK,' he says, 'you'll have to work damn hard: on call on alternative days and nights, and on call one weekend in two.'

I leave and once I arrive home, I ring Dan. He is at dinner with Sanda and Harry. He is all full of enthusiasm at the prospect.

'Did you ask how much you will be earning?' he asks. 'Once you have a residency visa, it will all be easier. I can get a job much quicker.'

'How about Nicky? If I take this job, I will need someone to look after her.'

'We'll discuss it next, when I am over. In the meantime, you make sure you get the job.'

'So be it,' I say. My voice sounds dead tired. I notice on the table a letter addressed to me and I open it. It is from the school. The headmistress calls me in to discuss Nicky's progress. It is their opinion that Nicky should repeat the school year. Although her language skills, reading and writing came up to a very good standard, her general school knowledge is behind. I feel so guilty; this is all my fault. I was so wrapped up in my own learning that I did not - and often I could not - help her with history, geography, RE and all the other subjects suitable for a nine-year-old. And now, if I take this job, I will be away from home a lot of the time. What was I thinking? What did I let myself into when I left Dimona?

Dan arrives the following Friday night. He insists that this is the right way to proceed and that I should write a letter of resignation to the polyclinic in Dimona.

'Trust me,' he says. 'You see how far we've got by following my advice. We got our freedom. Our child will grow up in a free country, and she'll follow her heart and mind without fear and discrimination.'

I don't know what to say. I would like to stay, live and work here. I like the atmosphere, the unobtrusive way in which people behave, the way they talk and do not dismiss you with indifference or rudeness when you ask something. When you go to a shop and someone is in front of you, they don't bang the door in your face, but they look behind and hold the door for you. I like my neighbours who proved to be so helpful and continue to be so. I like what London has to offer: museums, theatres, cinemas and good television programmes. I would like to work in the hospitals here; I have a lot to learn about modern facilities and, above all, about the consideration and respect for the patients that they all have.

But the journey to the east of London is difficult, and it takes such a long time. It's going to be such hard work and I cannot see how I could look after Nicky.

When and how will we function again as a family? Dan says that Nicky should go to a boarding school – at least for a year, till we are settled. She will catch up with what she has missed in her schoolwork, and learn better manners, the English way, and how to play hockey and rounders like a proper English girl. Later in life she will have all the opportunities; all the doors will open for her.

So I have failed my daughter again: I failed as a mother; I am too busy, too impatient, and I lack the knowledge to help my child. Dan ignores all this; he says that I have become oversensitive and that I overreact. Isn't this the kind of life that we dreamt about, the final goal? I am not sure anymore. I am harassed and uncertain of my own feelings, and I have no one to turn to for advice. So I go along with what he says. For the time being Nicky is going to France with him for the summer holidays. Dan sets out to find a suitable school for Nicky. Neither of us asks her how she feels about this decision. It is not in our upbringing to involve children in the parents' decisions.

Dan finds a boarding school for girls in Abbott's Hill, a village north, on the outskirts of greater London, part of the Girls' School Trust. He belongs to that group as an honorary girl, since he was a pupil in a girls' school that belonged to that trust, during the war. The school is in a grand mansion set in acres of woodland. I let Dan deal with it. I lack the willpower and strength to make any decisions. I write a letter of resignation to my polyclinic director and several letters to my uncles and cousins. It is not easy to explain but they seem to understand and wish us luck.

That is it. March on! Another chapter - another fragment of our life - starts right now!

32
WORK AND PLAY

Summer is wet and oppressive; the people around me call it hot, but I don't seem to find the heat. The blank white sky matches my mood. I spend alternative days on duty and I have my room in the hospital. It is large and comfortable, simply furnished but clean. Nicky spends the half-term at the end of May with me at the hospital. Nobody seems to mind. She spends time in the children's ward and makes friends with the older children. She also joins their lessons in the hospital's school. I wonder why nobody ever thought of that in Romania, particularly when some children spend long spells in hospital, some even being abandoned there. They simply lie there, confined to their beds, looking at the ceiling. Some parents came to visit, bringing food; others didn't bother.

My language and understanding are improving faster than when I was at the language school. I get on fine with the patients, perhaps due to my natural empathy with people who need me, but I communicate less well with the consultants and other people in authority. I am so eager not to make mistakes that I don't dare to voice any thoughts or opinions. I don't get on very well with the registrar, Dr Singh, particularly since he said in front of everyone that I got the job not on merit, but because

I am Jewish and so are most of the consultants. He is obsessed with race and persecution.

On my free weekends Nicky and I go out. We visit the National Gallery, and say hello to the old King Henry and other older kings and queens. We go to the British Museum, where Nicky is very interested in the mummies. Many a time our travels by public transport are fraught with difficulties. There is an Irish problem going on, which spreads gradually into London: bombs left in rubbish bins, in public places, stations evacuated and travel interrupted for hours.

One Saturday afternoon we set out to visit the Planetarium. We board the train at Wimbledon station at about 11 a.m. Just before the train stops at Charing Cross station, a message comes through the train's speakers: words appear hurried and slurred, and I cannot understand them. Once the train has stopped, we alight on to the platform and I see everyone running. Londoners are always rushing, so we keep walking the length of the platform and begin to cross the large concourse towards the exit without undue haste. Suddenly, a powerful arm grips my shoulder. I turn to face a policeman, who says: 'What do you think you are doing, Madam? Didn't you hear the announconcrete?'

I look around me, bewildered. The concourse is unusually empty. Indeed, all those people who were running seem to have vanished. Nicky squeezes my hand tight and I cannot find anything to say.

He pulls me hurriedly away and I narrowly avoid stepping over a brown parcel left alone, abandoned in the empty hall. The big burly man guides us without any further comment towards the exit, and once out of the station, he leaves us there, turns and rushes to join his colleagues. We notice a fire engine and an ambulance parked on the pavement. A member of staff stands by the entrance and informs whoever wants to enter the station that it is closed. When asked when it is going to be reopened, he says that he does not know. When somebody asks him why the station is closed, he tells them that there is a suspicious package found unattended and that the station will reopen only after the bomb disposal unit have finished with it and have given the all-clear. I wonder if it is the package I stumbled across and nearly fell over when we reached the concourse. *That would put an end to my dilemma;* the thought enters my mind and leaves it immediately. Nicky and I find a bus to Bakerloo Street and go to see the Planetarium.

During the summer Nicky is in France with her Daddy and spends most of the time with Sanda. Dan telephones every other evening, when he knows I am in my room, and I speak with him before Nicky takes over. She wants to know how her friends from the hospital are, especially little Abigail. Have they gone home or are they still in their beds? Abigail has a chronic incurable condition called Tay-Sacks and is going to spend the remainder of her life in hospital. I don't say this to Nicky.

It is almost 11 o'clock on a Saturday night and I've been on duty since the previous morning. With a bit of luck, I'll have a quiet night. Time for my last night round and then I hope that I will get some sleep.

One patient, Mr Gaugh, was unsettled the last time I saw him, in the afternoon. Sister May is on night duty. She phoned a few hours ago and I agreed to increase Mr Gaugh's sedation.

Later on, I enter the ward and indeed I find Mr Gaugh still unhappy. He complains of feeling sick. I don't dare add anything to his medication. I think I should ring the consultant. Oh, how I hate the telephone! I'd better prepare what I have to say to him. Dr Gordon answers almost immediately. I explain as best as I can what I have done and ask for his advice. In order to make myself understood, I speak louder than is necessary, and I see that Sister and some of the patients are following the conversation intently.

Then Dr Gordon says something very odd. 'Come down,' he says. I wonder how he has had time to arrive - or was he already in his consulting room downstairs? What's he doing here so late?

Obediently, I put the phone down and walk out of the ward. The lift does not seem to be working, so I rush down three flights of stairs as fast as I can. It does not do to keep the consultant waiting. Downstairs it's all quiet and there is no sign of Dr Gordon. I knock at the door of his consulting room but there is no reply. I run quickly to the mess in case he is there. Nothing. I rush back to the receptionist's counter, which is near the entrance. She lifts her eyes from the magazine that she is reading.

'Ah,'ere you are!' she says. 'You vanished. Doctor G is on and 'e wants to speak to ye.'

I realise that something is amiss and that I, somehow, have made a mistake. I take the receiver from her and say hello.

'Hello again,' Dr Gordon says. 'We've been interrupted. No matter.'

I mumble something in reply; I don't know what to say. He gives me the instructions and the advice I had asked for, and he wishes me a good, peaceful night. I thank him and return to the ward, where I make a note in the patient's record, write up his new medication, say goodnight and go to my room. Back in there, I put a call through to Dan, who is home looking after Nicky. I explain to him what happened. He takes a moment and then starts laughing.

'You silly woman!' he says. 'Doctor Gordon most likely said "calm down" not "come down". You must've misunderstood.'

'That makes sense,' I say with a sigh and go to bed.

33
THE FASSINAS

The six-month contract passes so quickly that I don't have time to catch my breath. Once I've embarked on the task, I throw myself into it with all my strength. I need to prove myself to the consultants and I need to prove Dr Singh wrong. His comment in the mess, the day I was appointed, still hurts. I should have said something but I did not make a sound and I did not repeat it to anyone. I do not have the courage to complain. Perhaps because I have been raised with discrimination, I am accustomed to take insults without replying. Maybe I half-believed him? Perhaps it is because I feel that I have just joined the team and I am in danger of creating a rift between the consultant and the registrar and the other members of the team. I am frightened and unsure of myself. So I set out to prove him wrong, although it's true that there are lots of things I don't know. So I avoid asking him. Instead, I find great support in Dr Fassina. He is so funny; when he has to perform a detailed procedure, he takes his glasses off. He is happy to advise and comes in, if necessary, to lend his expertise, provided that I do not call him during pub opening times. That's because he loves a drink - or not so much the drink as the company of pub drinkers. Maybe the fact that he was an outsider when he settled in

Britain makes him more sympathetic. Not long after I started my job, he invited me to have dinner with him and his wife.

To my surprise I find that my Spanish colleague, Maria Carmel from the language school, is there and that she started working in Dr Fassina's team at the German hospital where he is also a part-time consultant. I was a little apprehensive before I arrived; I had never before been invited by a consultant to his private home. That is not something that happens in Romania, where consultants or professors are put on pedestals like gods.

Dr Fassina lives with his partner, who is a senior nurse, in two rooms above a GP surgery that belongs to a friend, in the East End of London. During the meal of spaghetti Bolognese and lots of red wine, he tells us, when prompted by his wife, how he came to settle in England. He graduated as a doctor in Ontario just before the war and enrolled as a volunteer, joining a combat unit in Europe. He was eager for adventure. He fought in France and later in Italy. He ended the war at Monte Cassino, where he was asked to be an army translator, as Italian was his mother tongue. He was demobilised in London and stayed on; he said that he had had enough of seeing the world and travelling. He worked at St Steven's Hospital in Chelsea and he won a scholarship for his PhD in Pathology. He embraced London life and threw himself headlong into the whirl of clubs, pubs and debating societies. He became a Fabian, a friend of actors and painters and writers and women! He was a member of the Pen and Wig club. It was as if he were trying to live and make up for the time lost during the war. He was highly appreciated at work but when it came to acquiring a full consultancy, he was overlooked. He remained an outsider, good enough to be a long-term locum consultant but never nominated for a definitive post.

Our first encounter with his wife is fraught with difficulties and mistrust. Joy gives me and Maria furtive looks and watches every word we exchange with the doctor, who insists we call him Rene. I find this informal approach rather difficult. As the evening progresses, the atmosphere thaws a little and Joy starts talking about herself and Rene. She tells us how she met him.

Joy was a young nurse and a widow when she first met him. Her husband, a young lawyer, had died of tuberculosis. Grieving and lonely, she could not cope with the oppressive atmosphere in her mother-in-law's house, where she previously lived with her husband. She moved out and rented a small flat in Chelsea, just behind St Stephen's Hospital, where she was working. She met Rene while he worked as a senior registrar, studying for his PhD.

Joy, the daughter of a medical officer in India, was the product of a gentle generation of well-to-do officers' wives, who was educated at Cheltenham

Ladies' College. She was sent 'home' to study and was taught the rules of social etiquette. She had never met anyone like Rene before. His free spirit, colourful language and disregard for convention overwhelmed her. He was good-looking, with curly black hair, but he had lost those features with the passing of time. Indeed, he looks different to the pictures that Joy is showing us. He used to smoke cigars. She followed him everywhere and shared his whirlwind lifestyle. After two years she moved in with him, sharing the small shabby apartment above a doctor's surgery in the East End. They did not marry; Rene did not believe in that institution. The hospital gossip, Dr Singh, is convinced that Dr Fassina has left behind in Canada a wife and at least four children.

Perhaps, I thought, not being married to him makes Joy so insecure. It is from her that I learn that drinking water from a wine glass is an insult to civilisation. She insists that you cut and stab with your fork small morsels of meat, and then cover them, with the help of your knife, with peas and carrots and potatoes, all mushed up. She gets so annoyed when Rene refuses to conform to her pretentious demands; he continues to cut his meat with the knife in the right hand and the fork in the left, before changing them over so that he can pick up his food with the fork in his right hand. For Joy this is such an important issue that I make sure that I don't use the fork like a scoop either, as I am used to, so as not to add to her displeasure. But Rene does not care. Rene likes to keep an open house and forever invites friends to dinner and drinks, and Joy loves it, even though she keeps complaining. She still works at St Stephen's and has to leave early in the morning to make the tedious journey from Stratford to Chelsea.

Once Joy feels reassured that I am not a threat, we become friends. I visit them often and have a meal with them or go to the pub. When Dan comes over, they both take an instant liking to him, and Rene, with his innate enthusiasm, sets out to look among his numerous friends to find a job suitable for Dan. We drink whisky, beer and wine; we meet all sorts of people from the East End: Harry, an ex-boxer who used to be a bodyguard for the Kray brothers, is a polite softly spoken man who couldn't hurt a fly; a New Zealander dentist obsessed with rugby and heavy drinking; a few actors like Stephen Lewis from *On the buses*; a few well-known writers; and a few stall holders from the Romney market. The sort of people I would never have rubbed shoulders with in my previous life.

At work I find him a good teacher. He is not particularly liked by the other consultants, probably because of his accent, the way he speaks using a lot of 'goddamn it!' and the people he mixes with. All the other consultants are part of the high class establishment, the polite people.

One Wednesday afternoon we have an outpatient clinic. There are appointments made for new patients, as well as follow-ups for the people recently discharged from hospital or due for review of long-standing conditions.

I have my own consulting room, and I see people who were already assessed by the consultant and treated. I discuss progress since the patient was last seen, review their medication, examine them and give follow-up appointments. There is a nurse at hand who weighs the patients, checks their blood pressure and urine, and sorts out any tests that I wish to request from the lab. If there are any doubts, I pop in and out of the consultant's room. It is a wonderful system and my thoughts go back to the poor unfortunate people from my previous hospitals, whom I or my colleagues discharged and abandoned to their fate, never to be seen again, unless they had to be readmitted as an emergency. The feeling that people are not abandoned, that someone cares, is such a good feeling.

On Thursday morning there is the ward round with the consultant, the registrar, the ward Sister and me. One of these Thursdays, after the ward round, Dr Fassina asks me to meet him at lunchtime to go out on a visit. Of course, I do as I am told. On the way out he tells me that Mrs Elsie Jacobs, whom we admitted the previous evening, lives alone and that she has a cat. The only way she would agree to come in was if Dr Fassina promised that he would take care of the cat. That is where we are going. I cannot believe my ears but I just can't stop admiring the man's sense of humanity. We arrive on this narrow street with a row of small houses and tiny front gardens, not far from the River Lee. He feeds the cat and then takes me on a tour along the Thames canal, along the quay of the old East India Docks. Large warehouses stand abandoned and look almost sinister, with their barbed wire and corrugated iron shutters. Some have been broken into and the gaps make them look like large toothless mouths. The water in the canals is murky and stale. These places were once teeming with trade from the Far East: ships and barges, dredges and labourers. Now it is all abandoned. But Dr Fassina is interested in them and their story, and he says that if he could, he would buy a wharf in Bromley Marsh or near Blackwall. I say nothing, as buying abandoned wharfs is not my priority at present, but I learn things about London that I've never known. And of course we walk on, along the Thames, and end up in the Mayflower pub. I hear the story of the Pilgrim Fathers who set off from this point to spread the word of God in America.

34
KEEP YOUR HANDS BY YOUR SIDE

Summer came and it is on its way out, and I barely noticed it. First of all, because it wasn't much of a summer, the way I understand it. Secondly, because I miss Nicky. We speak on the phone often and she does not complain, except for the fact that Aunt Sanda insists that she eats everything on her plate, even if she does not like it. Dan repeats everything that Sanda says. This eating everything often makes Nicky sick.

I reassure her by saying, 'Don't worry, darling, soon you'll be back home,' knowing full well that on her return, she will go to boarding school. So I immerse myself in work.

I am back at work after a week off because my back went. It was a most painful but at the same time most enlightening experience. It happened during the morning ward round exactly a week previously. It was a Thursday. We moved from bed to bed: Dr Fassina followed by the registrar, Dr Singh, on one side of the bed and me, taking notes of what I would have to do after the round, on the other side. Sister was standing next to me, as is the custom, a few paces behind. We were round Mrs Strobosky's bed, an elderly lady, grossly overweight, who suffered a stroke the previous day. Dr Fassina started to talk to the registrar about her, her diabetes and all her other problems.

The patient suddenly moved on to her good side, with her back towards me and Sister, nearing the edge of the bed. The conversation between consultant and registrar went on and on. The lady, restless and confused, turned again on her back and further towards the abyss. Horror of horrors, I could see it coming. In a split second, I instinctively put my hands out to catch her. She fell with all her weight on to my arms and sent me to the ground. Everybody started running to help us. They lifted the patient off me and then, with some help, I stood up.

Initially, I did not think there was anything wrong, but late that afternoon I found that I couldn't move. My back was alive with pain. I couldn't breathe. The porter took me in a wheelchair to my room. Dr Fassina gave me painkillers and a sedative. And for about three days I was in that prostate state. However, I was told that I am not entitled to medical leave. The accident form was filled by the nursing staff but I am refused paid leave on the grounds that it was not in my job description to lift patients. I should have called for the porters.

I do not mind because I didn't know the procedure and, even if I had been aware of it, I do not think it would have worked in that particular case. I didn't expect anything. If this had happened in Romania, I would not even have thought of compensation. However, all the staff were very helpful: the radiologist x-rayed my back, the physio gives me a few sessions, and the consultant treats me and looks after me without any fuss.

Now I am able to stand up and I return to my duties.

35
ONE JOB FINISHES, ANOTHER STARTS

I fill in application forms. I write my professional story again and again. Sometimes I get a reply: 'Thank you, but no thanks.' Most often I don't get any reply at all. I apply to any advertisement for a senior house officer job in and around London. After about 60 such letters I receive five invitations for interviews: Watford, Luton, Southend, Mill Hill and Whipps Cross in Leytonstone.

After the interviews, I fill in more forms - for expenses and transport reimbursement. There is no repayment for the heartache and disappointment or fear for the uncertain future. Dr Singh keeps repeating, 'Don't bother. If there is a single English doctor applicant among the ones invited for interview, you must know that the job is theirs. You might as well start filling in the expenses form.'

I don't know if this is entirely true - at least I hope it's not - but it increasingly looks that way. I do not visit hospitals before the interviews or meet the consultants, the way my colleagues advise me to do. Nor do I ask any questions during the interview. I worry that questioning the interviewers is rude. I don't know how to look eager and show them that I am interested. I just answer their questions the best I can. I would like to get a job in paediatrics. At least I will learn something entirely new.

At last I get a job at Whipps Cross Hospital. This is the district hospital which serves the part of the East End of London, the cradle for immigrants. It is near Leytonstone Station. On the Underground it will take me more than an hour from Wimbledon.

The ugly, red Victorian building, spread out on a large area, is surrounded by scaffolding and construction equipment. A new maternity unit is being built on a rise within the hospital's grounds about half a mile away from the main building. I am the new SHO, the newest addition to the children department's team. Dr Hinden is the consultant in charge: an elderly gentle giant who reminds me of a teddy bear. He is softly spoken, with an elegant accent revealing his upper class upbringing and education. Even I can, by now, make the distinction. Dr Willer is the senior registrar. It is with her that I will be working every day. She wears glasses and her hair is grey. She is very thin: her lips are thin and her nose is narrow. I think she goes once a week to have her hair set. I suspect that she is younger than she looks, as she has a somewhat old-fashioned way of dressing and talking. But she is very efficient and most concerned with the work at hand, which she attacks with determination and precision.

There is plenty of work. I've never seen so many sick children. They come in continuously, day and night, through emergency admissions. Meningitis and meningitis septicaemia are the greatest problems this late autumn. I am on call every other night and day, and I barely have time to go to my room. I've promised Nicky that I will write every day but I sometimes forget. When I get to my room, my eyes close with tiredness. The smell of curry and garlic greets me at the door, for my room is in a prefab building which I share with four other colleagues. There is a communal kitchen and bathroom, and two toilets. Some of the Asian doctors are not keen on the shepherd's pie or the stew from the hospital canteen and prefer to cook for themselves. I get friendly with another doctor who is part of the same team as me. She is from Hyderabad and wears lively coloured saris. One weekend, when we have a little break, she teaches me how to fold the 12 pleats of the material and pin it at the end with a large safety pin. I didn't know that Hindu religion forbids the sewing of garments. I am learning something new every day. In the room next to mine is a colleague I've met before at the London Hospital. He was working as an SHO in the surgical team there and here he is attached to the medical team. He is from Pakistan and, like me, he has to pass the final exams to obtain full registration. He tells me that his wife and children are still back home and I wonder why most nights, when I am trying to sleep, his bed is squeaking rhythmically, and there are giggles and sighs coming from his room. I must tell him to oil the joints of the bed.

In the wards, the Sisters seem to keep their distance and address me as Dr Vicks, while they are on first-name terms with my Indian colleague and the registrar. They begin to be a little friendlier the day I find them all lined up, sitting on every available chair, each with a baby in her arms, bottle-feeding them. I ask if I can join them and they say, 'Of course,' and smile. They talk about everything that happened in the last 24 hours, at their home or in the hospital. I don't join in, just listen, and none of them ask me anything beyond: 'Where are you from?' Perhaps this is because I am the only one of the team who cannot speak proper English - or could it be that perhaps my eyes suggest that I am frightened to be addressed? There is one person, though, who seems to get close to me: the social worker attached to the team. Her name is Clare: she is American and each time I meet her, she seems to be interested and starts chatting to me. I tell her by the by that I have a daughter. One day she asks me if I would like to meet her after work. There is a little pub outside the hospital that she recommends. I am happy and agree, and we meet the following Monday. I am looking forward to seeing a friendly person.

She orders coffee for both of us and an orange juice. There are few customers in the pub and we can talk. I soon realise where the conversation is leading: she wants to know if I am happy being separated from my daughter, whether I see my husband and how I am coping. In other words, I realise that she is conducting a social worker's interview. All of a sudden, I become less communicative: I recoil and refuse to be drawn into further disclosures. I find the leading questions arrogant and intrusive. An uneasy silence follows, and she pays for the coffee and we part company. When we meet again, she ignores me.

With the approaching of winter, work becomes busier and more intense. There is a surge of meningitis cases, and the children and babies come in very ill.

I've done a few lumbar punctures in my time but this is the first time that I have to perform this procedure on babies or toddlers. I shake and shiver, and work myself into a state before I have to do it, making a supreme effort to keep my hand from shaking under the scrutinising eyes of the nurses. Only the Matron, Elsie, is encouraging. Once I've done a few, I become more relaxed.

When I am on call, which means an 18-hour shift without much respite, I am to attend the Accident & Emergency department. There is no separate medical cover there. I see children as they come in: whooping cough, asthma and bronchiolitis. Some parents speak less English than I do or with an accent that makes it difficult to understand. Some parents don't allow certain procedures due to religious taboos; some refuse any injections or blood to be given to their children, even when there is a desperate need to do so. I have to call Miss Wheeler for help, as I don't know all the legal implications. What I fail to understand is how some parents decide to refuse treatment for their children. More importantly, why do we allow it? Why do we let them do it? When we run out of options, we half-heartedly refer them to a court of law to decide. I don't know much about abused children and how to recognise them, but soon I get to know the familiar stare into a distant space - the lack of smile or cries of toddlers and babies who submit to our ministrations without protest.

36
HOW ABOUT A BIKE?

When on call, I have to cover any emergencies from the maternity unit. Some babies refuse to breathe after the birth or they slow down in the womb before they are born and they need to be intubated within three minutes of delivery, if they are to come out of this trauma undamaged.

I share these duties with the anaesthetist on call. He is a newly graduated young man from Sheffield. After the first week in his job, he comes out with a bright idea: 'What do you say if we buy or borrow a bike? There is no way we can reach the new maternity wing on time if we have to walk this long Victorian corridor.'

'You mean riding the bike inside the hospital?' I haven't ridden a bike since my father caught me with my friend in the woods, getting lessons from some young officers in my hometown. I must have been 14 or 15.

'Why not?' he says. 'You could sit on the back or on the bar.' Why not, indeed... Learning, learning.

I encounter, understand and learn a wealth of new things. I am in a difficult position: I am older than the registrar and the other medical junior staff, with the exception of the matron and Dr Hinden, but I know less than them. I have the constant feeling that they look down on me, but I am determined to overcome this and prove myself. Dan says I am getting paranoid, and Rene and Joy, whom we visit often, encourage me. They think that soon I'll be ready to sit my first exam. My old friend Ursula is very good at helping me; she loves Nicky and often comes with me to take her out on my free weekends. Nicky is full of news: she already has friends and she brings them with her on our outings. She tells me that they play 'shops' in the woods and that she loves her cello. She has discovered a new talent. She likes to sew and is encouraged by her teacher. She has been voted the prettiest girl of her class and she is very pleased. In our last meeting, she was excited and she couldn't wait to share her news. She was chosen to be the mermaid queen in the play that the class is preparing for the Christmas celebrations. She also tells me, in a matter-of-fact way, that one of her new friends, Elly, kissed her on the neck and back while having a shower. Ursula looks at me horrified.

Ursula has no children and she is so Swiss! I suggest to Nicky that the next time I come to see her she should invite Elly to come out with us. Nicky agrees, not showing much interest.

When we meet again, Nicky brings Elly. She is a sweet child, small and thin, with enormous vivid blue eyes. She comes from Australia: she is an only child and her parents recently moved to England. It seems to me that she is lonely and lost, and is happy to have a friend. When Dan comes at the weekend, I tell him about this and we both agree that there is nothing to worry about: there are many ways in which nine-years-olds express and forge friendships.

Not long after, I am on call again; it is my turn for a long weekend. I long for a free weekend. But it is Monday morning and I admit a two-year-old child. His father is carrying him. His baby's cheeks are a mosaic of bruises in various shades of blue, changing into green and yellow. A hush descends upon us all in A&E: concerned stares, meaningful exchanges of glances – a negative feeling prevails. We look at the father with resentment, almost hatred. How could he? We've already made not only a diagnostic, but we have also made up our minds: guilty! This is a battered child, poor little creature! We are the judge, jury and prosecutor. *'J'accuse!'* we cry in our voiceless voice and call the police. Mum is upset; the father is scared.

Then an outsider, Denise, who just joined our team, replacing my Indian friend who had completed her contract, comes up with another point of view. 'Let's have some blood tests.'

Within hours we have the results. Leukaemia is shouting at us through each of the bruises. Our stares change from anger to concern. We no longer accuse the parents but rush to comfort the mother and father, all in the space of a few minutes. I don't know about the others, but I feel embarrassed and promise myself never to point the accusing finger to anyone before investigating and making sure that I know all the facts - and that they are correct.

But in among the children that come and go there is the odd baby or toddler who stares quietly into the distant space, lies absolutely still and speaks little, if at all. The baby who has long ago, almost since birth, given up all the hope with which he entered the world, as it was beaten out of him. It is my task, together with everyone else who cares, to save this baby.

One night I receive a call from the maternity unit. My friend, the anaesthetist, presents himself to A&E, complete with bike, and together we make our way to maternity. He is pedalling furiously. I sit on the bar, obstructing his field of vision. A premature baby is making his way out into the world. His mother is very ill and a Caesarean section is in progress.

He is a little boy who weighs 1.4 kg. He comes out silently. I apply suction and he is intubated: finally, he gives a weak cry which then fades away. We try again to revive him but there is no sign of life, we all agree. It is my job to inform the father. He cries and I utter words of comfort. I do the same a few hours later, when the mother is awake. The two hold on tight to each other and I sit with them for a while, hoping that my blip will not ring and disturb. After a while, the mother asks to see her little boy: it is their first child and she wants to hold him. I speak with the obstetrician and we agree. I go to find the baby, who by now has been taken away into a side ward, from where the mortuary porter will collect him. I enter the room and I think I must be mistaken, but from the small cot, under the sheets, I can hear a weak cry. A little fearful, I approach and remove the cover… and there he is: the prem is alive! I dial with trembling hands Dr Hinden's number; luckily, he is in the hospital. Then I ring the neonatal ward, asking for an emergency incubator, oxygen and everything else. I apply myself to cleaning the baby's mouth and wrap him up to prevent further loss of heat. I manage to listen to his heart, which is very fast - but that's OK for a newborn - when the doors burst open and everyone else takes over. Soon he is restored to life and upgraded from a stillbirth to a human. All that remains to be done is for someone to go and inform the parents. After a long debate, the task seems to fall on me, as I was the one who confirmed his death and found him alive. I feel I could do with a strong drink but there is none. I cannot wait to go home.

Tuesday morning and I am back to work, refreshed after a night's sleep, but another problem awaits. The auxiliary staff are on strike over pay and conditions. We all agree with them, but the immediate problem is that we don't have ice for the humidifying tents. These are used to help children in severe breathing distress. The porters, who usually bring the ice to the ward, are outside the hospital, picketing. We organise a rota and do the job ourselves as best we can.

There are good weeks and not so good ones.

37
A DIFFICULT WEEK

On a Friday afternoon, just at the time when I was ready to go home, there is an emergency. My colleague who is taking over from me has her hands full and I have to stay behind. A 12-year-old boy is brought in by his uncle. The uncle, a local Walthamstow man in his thirties, tells me that as far as he knows the boy had a fall at school. When questioned closely, the boy, who seems very upset, says that he was running a race and when he reached the end, he hit his head hard on the wall at the finishing line. He says that it didn't hurt and he didn't faint. The uncle tells me that once home, the boy's mother found that his behaviour had changed. Normally a nice kid, he became aggressive and shouted most unpleasant swear words, to the point that she had to call on the uncle who brought him in. I send for an x-ray and admit him for observation, although the first x-ray did not show a fracture or any abnormality of the head.

I leave and that weekend we go to visit the newly opened safari park somewhere north of Watford. Dan drives his blue Fiat; after picking up Nicky from Abbott's Hill School we drive on through miles and miles of green fields and lovely small villages.

The following Monday I start the week on duty, and I understand that my colleague had a rough weekend - mostly with the boy, who deteriorated. He is now semi-conscious and vomiting. The consultant came in twice during the weekend and no diagnosis has been made so far. All investigations proved useless. By midday the boy is dead. The atmosphere in the ward turns from white to black with mourning.

As it falls again on me to inform the family, I am told that the boy's father is in prison and therefore I will have to contact the official channels of authority. It's a most unpleasant experience. I have to repeat the terrible story to each officer at every level, as if climbing up a ladder. I never get to speak to the father, but I convey my condolences through the prison's governor.

Late that afternoon, a post mortem is organised and we all want to be there. A hairline skull fracture that could not be detected by x-ray and a consequent bleed is the verdict.

A small man with dark-skin complexion and jet-black hair walks into A&E and I am on call, yet again. In his arms he carries a thin girl who appears to be asleep. To my obvious introductory question, he replies briefly, in his stilted accent: 'Piss too much!'

It is all the information he can give but it is enough. I need to check a urine sample and this confirms what I had already guessed. I am dealing with a diabetic child who is in a coma. Even before I get the results, I set up a drip and work out the insulin dose required, should the diagnostic be confirmed. I feel good for having done something right. I admit the child in the ward just as she regains consciousness.

38
A NEW PLAN OF ACTION

Junior jobs in NHS hospitals are as such that from the moment one starts a new job, one already has to think of what comes next - the next assignment - knowing that six months or a maximum of 12 will pass quickly. With that in mind, one starts scanning the BMJ job section - a bit casually at first but as time passes, more and more intensely.

There are two possible outcomes: a) the next job will be a step up the ladder towards achieving the ultimate goal of becoming a consultant or b) the next assignment will be 'Where is the next slice of bread coming from?' If the former is what happens then all is well. That will lead to the next step: how to get a job in a prestigious hospital, where one could get a push further up the ladder.

If the goal is simply to earn a crust, then any job with improved pay will do. There are lots of small marginal hospitals that do not have the status of leading teaching hospitals. Some are very busy, with a wealth of 'hands-on' opportunities for practical experience, whereas others are quiet and dull. Those have a positive side: there is plenty of time to study, pass exams, look after the family, and so on. Most applicants for such jobs are women or immigrants.

The people who go for top jobs aim to reach the position of consultants, where one is set for life. No more research papers, challenges or community voluntary projects designed to secure prestigious positions. From then on, it is plain sailing for them: time is their own to give themselves and the patients the time they need. They benefit from pharmaceutical companies' free lunches and trips abroad; and they can play golf or pursue any other hobbies that take their fancy. Unfortunately, such jobs are few and far between. So, senior registrars, at the top of the junior staff ladder, get grey hair and sour dispositions while waiting for a consultant vacancy. Year after year they cannot settle into marriage, have children or buy a house of their own, in case the job becomes available somewhere else.

The second solution is to abandon the chase and, once the training is complete, go into General Practice. The glamour is taken off the career but there is stability; one starts a business or enters in a partnership with other doctors, choosing hours to suit. However, the responsibility for the patient is 24 hours a day. A general practitioner gets to know the families and their way of life, and has the time to build his or her own family. A general practitioner becomes a respected member of their local community, rubbing shoulders with the vicar and the mayor. One is set for life. You join a practice, and your partners become your brothers and sisters; you are married to the practice. It does not take me long to learn all this and know what path I am going to take.

The six-month job finally comes to end. I am asked if I want to apply for another job, one grade up. Dr Hinden seems to appreciate my efforts and the progress I've made, and the matron, Elsie, who supported me from the start, encourages me to stay. But I feel that I cannot keep up the pace. These six months were some of the most interesting of my career: I've learned such a lot. But the price is too high. My daily headache has become a fixture and my nights are disturbed by nightmares even when I am not at work. I start applying again for jobs. By now I am an expert at filling forms, collecting character references and being prepared to wait.

There is some good news. Rene has kept his word and made enquiries about finding a job for Dan: one of his friends, who owns a small factory in Dartford which produces machine tools, may be interested in offering Dan a job. Not long after, Rene arranges a meeting. We are invited for Sunday lunch, together with Rene and Joy, at this man's residence somewhere in Kent.

39
SOME GOOD, SOME BAD

The bad news is that I get a telephone call from Nicky's school. The headmistress wants to speak to us, the parents. I take a day off and go to Abbott's Hill. The nearest train station is Kings Langley. Nicky and another friend have made an attempt to run away from school. The two girls were found in the woods on the school grounds. I am horrified. I put a call through to Dan and share my news. He appears the next morning, having driven through the night. We talk about Nicky, whom we know is not a complainer, and wonder why she has never said how unhappy she was. I didn't really think that she wanted to run away. All she wanted was to come home. I leave Dan to deal with it and take the train back to work. I am thinking that soon will be Christmas and Nicky will be on leave. I take the next weekend off and we go together to Paris. The sea is rough and the hovercraft is wobbling up and down, moving with the high waves. Nicky is sick all the way and I feel sick. I don't dare look through the portholes where one minute I can see the sky and the next we are underwater. Dan seems unperturbed; he orders a whisky and a newspaper.

We are excited: Dan's parents are expected to arrive. Their visa was granted a month ago and they finally managed to leave Romania. They chose to stay with Amy (Dan's younger sister), who married a Frenchman. The family lives in Lille. Tears and kisses and hugs: Christmas Eve is more festive than ever in Jean Renaud's house. We are hungry for their news, and news about our friends and my family. We want to know if life has changed since we've left.

'Yes, it has. And not for the better,' they say. Shortages of food and everyday essentials have increased. The country exports almost everything it produces. It is the leader's idea of 'independence'. We don't want to owe anybody anything, so the price is paid, as usual, by the population. Only chicken wings and bones are allowed to be sold in the shops, while chickens travel far and wide to foreign markets. Coffee is sold with a mixture of hay and barley grains, hence its new nickname of *neigh-coff* (an anagram suggestive of horse food). Hospitals are ill-equipped; there is no longer a training programme for nurses and social workers, and food for patients is provided by individual members of the patient's family. Heating in the majority of Stalinist-type high-rise buildings is coming from a central station and in winter the room temperature is set everywhere at below 18°C. The discontent is mounting but it does not affect the ones in power, who create increasing privileges for themselves. It appears that my parents have finally made the decision to apply for a visa to go to Israel, as my sister Bea has finished her studies and has already left. The festive atmosphere is slightly awkward due to the fact that Jean Renaud and his widowed mother do not understand our language but on the whole everyone is jolly with the help of French wine and admirable food. After the parents retire, we have a little talk with JR and Amy, and agree that when the new immigrants recover from their ordeal, we must make a concerted effort to help them regain their independence. Years of living with the younger members of the family and depending on them made them slightly fearful of facing everyday life on their own. JR promises to put them in touch with all the official support organisations, as age is against them in terms of employment.

Later on they will settle in Paris, where they are given an apartment in a tall council-owned building in one of the *banlieues,* and George will get a job as a researcher at the National Library. We return to England, after the long time it took Nicky to finally part from her grandparents. She obviously missed them and they missed her. She wants to tell them all about her new friends, England, school and everything else.

40
DAN GETS A JOB

Dan comes to England a fortnight later and I can't wait to tell him the news. We are going to meet Mr Collins on Sunday. We are invited, together with Rene and Joy, to spend a day at his farm. I make a point not to forget to have a chat with Joy before the visit and find out a little more about this Mr Collins. Dan says that I shouldn't bother.

'If he hires me, that's good enough for me - as long as I can set foot in England, secure a job and get permission to stay. After that we'll see. If it doesn't work, I will move to the next job.'

I admire his confidence, his pragmatic approach. Nothing deters him from what he wants. He gives me the strength I do not possess. I rely on him to make the right decisions.

He says that if Nicky can't be looked after properly, she is to stay at the boarding school at Abbott's Hill till such time when we both have jobs and a home. Then she can come home.

'Like a puppet on a string'; 'We dance to the music of time' - silly snatches of music pop into my mind for no apparent reason.

It all happens at once. The visit to the farm is a success. Ray Collins's wife laid out a lovely dinner: a whole cod on a platter, swimming in egg mayonnaise, accompanied by plenty of drinks. It is a sunny afternoon and we are invited to do a spot of gardening. Ray is eager to show off his new lawnmower with a seat, so he can drive it around the large estate. I am trimming the lawn's edges, round the flower beds. Joy is flirting with the men, rolling her eyes and skipping barefoot on the grass.

I am beginning to settle; the tensions that built over the last year diminishes. I have more time to spend with Nicky. Bromley is a pleasant area and we rent an apartment just behind the GPO building, on St Ann's Avenue. Nicky finds a friend - a boy of the same age - and they spend the holiday off exploring together. The boy's parents rent the flat above ours, having recently returned from working abroad.

Once the formalities have been completed, Dan starts work. Dartford is not too far away, about ten miles - half an hour at the most by car.

'How was your day?' I ask, hoping that I will get more than the usual: 'It was OK.'

'The guys and the foreman look at me with suspicion, maybe resentment. I have made a work schedule for them, a time in motion, to avoid waste,' he says. 'I hope they will follow. Ray seems quite impressed.'

'Will you be in later?'

'Don't think so. Ray asked me to go with him to the pub. I'll have to go, I suppose.'

Almost at the same time, miracles happen, as they sometimes do. After my umpteen applications, I get a job: a part-time job or a job share is on offer. That must be a first in the medical training jobs. It is at Guy's Evelina Hospital for children, where I will be sharing with another doctor, who happens to be the wife of the prestigious hospital's governor. He is a retired general, an army doctor. At that time Guy's was a place where military medical personnel found training places and permanent positions after they finished their army contracts. Why I was chosen, I don't know. I was later to find out that one of the consultant's daughter-in-laws had recently had a baby and decided not to take the position at the last minute, and I was next on the list of choices.

This is ideal: I will work in the afternoon in children's casualty, have the morning to take Nicky to her new school and hopefully find some time to prepare for the exams. Just by chance one day I meet my colleague from the London Jewish and later from Whipps Cross. We decide to meet in a small café, together with Maria Carmel, the Spanish doctor who finished her contract at the German Hospital and is preparing to take her final exams for full registration. She still lives with the English family where she worked as a nanny since she came to England. The two children need her even more now, since their mother died. One morning the woman was found at the bottom of the stairs with a broken neck. The police were involved and Maria Carmel was questioned as a witness, but nothing else was heard. We change the subject. My Pakistani colleague is a mine of information. He knows all the ropes when it comes to how to get into the system. He plans to go to Dublin to take his finals, as reports are that they are easier over there. I cannot understand the point. Why go that far when there is an examination board in England at the Royal College of Physicians? I cannot grasp the idea that there is a difference between the toughness of exams between London, Edinburgh or Dublin. He passes the exam on his first attempt the following year, and later on I am to meet him again, a full consultant psychiatrist in the Midlands.

One weekend Dan suggests that we go to look at the shops. There is a large Army and Navy store in Bromley and also a superstore called Allders. Further down towards Bromley North station there are lots of small shops and antique furniture places. We find a small bric-a-brac shop and fall in love with two antique saddle chairs with nicely sculpted tiger heads at each end. Now that we have two useless chairs we may as well start looking for a house. These chairs cannot be used outside!

'Mammy, I want a dog!' Nicky greets us when we return. Her face is flushed and her breathing is fast as if she has been running. She and her friend have just returned after exploring the roof of the greenhouse, which almost collapsed under their weight.

The next time we meet with Joy and Rene, they take us to the flea market. Everything is for sale there: clothes new and not so new, tools, machinery, utensils, fruit and vegetables, flowers, and even live chickens, puppies and kittens. Nicky falls in love with a brown puppy with barely open eyes, no older than four or five weeks. The seller reassures us that it is healthy. On our way home we realise that the puppy is full of fleas and shivers a great deal. I put some bread and milk on a saucer in front of her, and she laps it up in no time and wants some more. The vet surgery is not far, at the other end of our street, and he can see us that same afternoon. We carry the puppy, who is really adorable, with her pink tummy swollen after all the food she has eaten. The vet gives her the first vaccine, flea sprays and deworming tablets, and Nicky is happy. She takes charge.

41
EVELINA HOSPITAL FOR CHILDREN

Life at Evelina, the paediatrics unit, is quite different from the district hospital. It is decidedly more stylish and refined. Guy's is a teaching hospital, and one of the main central hubs of medical excellence and teaching besides Bart's, King's College, St Thomas's, Westminster, St George's, UCL and St Mary Paddington. The old imposing building framed by colonnades is set in a small garden, where Lord Nuffield's statue stands. Behind the cloisters is the chapel where the remains of Sir Thomas Guy are buried. It is just a footbridge across from London Bridge train station. The deanery and medical school are at the back in another building.

Building materials are driven to and fro in big lorries; there is a lot of renewal in the area.

Evelina hospital for children is less than a mile away along the road, past the Greenwood pub and the now closed wholesale Borough market, near Southwark Bridge. It is a corner building on three floors, dedicated to children and their care. A few yards north, the roar of the trains can be deafening.

The ground floor is occupied by the Accident &Emergency where Iris, Jane and Nona reign supreme. They are the secretary, the admission clerk and administrator who adopted Evelina like one adopts a foster child. They have to know everything that's going on, pass comment on every parent that comes through the door, and offer their evaluation of the medical and nursing performance. It is wise to stay on the right side of them, but making friends is not easy. They greet the doctor who occupied the position I have now like a relative. She comes in with a Moses basket and her baby girl, all in pink. Her husband is a junior houseman in the hospital. He is the son of a consultant and has hopes of eventually taking his father's position, if and when the time comes.

The consultants are top professors of international standing. A large number of the junior doctors are sons and daughters of those consultants, who pass from one junior contract to another as they bide their time till the right job becomes available in their pursuit of the right career. So I mix with the best; they are very bright and well educated, and have what the French call 'savoir vivre' and Dan calls the right connections. The weekly meetings take place at the Greenwood pub, where cases are discussed. The table is buzzing with small talk, innuendoes, and discussions about music and theatre. The recent young graduates flirt with the consultants, and stories of mésalliances and love affairs float about. I am oblivious to many of those situations: I am not on the ball - an expression I have recently learned - and the jokes go above my head because I do not understand them, so I get a reputation as a dull, insipid person, although relations remain cordial. Like at the previous hospital, I remain Dr Vicks, while they all are John and Verity and Valerie, Jacinta and Phillip. I am happy to be here: it is so much easier to come at 1o'clock in the afternoon on weekdays and take over the job where my morning colleague left it. I have the morning to myself to take Nicky to school, cook a meal and do all the other domestic chores. I even have time to study a little. We discovered that there are some organisations that collected papers over the years with the most frequent subjects that were asked in the written paper and most frequent questions asked in the vivas.

My other working half, with whom I share duties, is the wife of the hospital governor, a recently retired army general. She has three teenage children and has many social duties besides medicine. She speaks the Queen's English with the exaggerations and the inflections belonging to the upper crust. We sit together for an hour, depending on how many patients are waiting to be seen, and she talks about the help that she is giving to her eldest daughter who is trying to sit the entrance exam to Medicine, the last posting that her husband had in Berlin and the new house that the family has acquired as part of this new posting, not far from the hospital in one of the exclusive squares. She speaks loudly and likes to have an audience, I notice, involving the three ladies who hang on to her every word. The only time she speaks quietly is when she is ready to impart a piece of gossip, in confidence. We discuss the patients she saw in the morning and she warns me in case some come back for further assessment. Sometimes, either because she forgets or due to a streak of competitiveness, she fails to pass on some important details, which puts me in a situation of disadvantage. I talk about this to Joy and she says that this is typical of army wives. She should know, as her mother was the wife of an army doctor.

The staff and surroundings are the top echelon; one of my consultants is a powerful politician who will in future become a minister. Another politician of great prestige and in the media spotlight comes one morning with his grandchild for some problems, and the nurses are eager to hear what he has to say about immigration and the strikes, but he says nothing and smiles paternally. The other patients are children who are not well; sometimes working with them is more difficult than dealing with the ones in the East End, because one has to be so very careful about what one says.

One thing I have to learn is not to take sides. When one day a mother comes in with her battered 18-month-old, it is so easy to hate her. The receptionist's eyes throw daggers at her as she sits with her head down and her cheeks stained by tears. One of the nurses barely talks to the mother. But the

Sister and the registrar want to get the story right. The mother, a pretty young woman and well educated, brings up the baby single-handedly. Her partner left when she was in the last term of her pregnancy. She has no money and her pride does not let her apply for state support. She copes the best she can by babysitting other children or knitting garments for a little wool shop near Elephant and Castle. She lost contact with her parents since her boyfriend came into her life and she got pregnant. I knew her because she visited on a few occasions during the previous weeks to seek advice for a cold and about suitable food for her little toddler. This morning she went out with the child in the pushchair to buy some food with the little money that she had. On the way home, she noticed that the baby girl had taken one of her boots off and had lost it. That was the last straw. She battered the child around the head: the cheeks were covered in bruises and she forcefully took her out the pushchair while the child was still strapped in, which caused a lot of damage on the legs. The child is admitted and the social worker is called to give support, as is the health visitor, who comforts the mother.

The other day, a well-dressed gentleman in his mid-forties brought in his son, a 12-year-old boy. The man seems irritable and in a hurry. 'I am here against my better judgement,' he says, 'but my wife has run out of patience with my son. You must forgive me, Doctor, I apologise in advance for wasting your time. My son refuses to go to school. It is now almost three months since all this started. If the nanny takes him to school, he will almost invariably be home by lunchtime because of migraine. The school phones and someone must go to fetch him. Once at home, he is all right. My wife and myself are busy people, you understand, and this is becoming most inconvenient. The family doctor cannot find anything wrong.'

The boy stands with his head down, a grim expression on his face.

'Hello Bill, I would like to examine you: nothing that will hurt or be unpleasant – just a few exercises,' I say, thinking that I should do a brief neurological examination.

One of my colleagues, Phillip, passes by and he wants a chat. The boy obediently bends down and takes his shoes off. I conduct the examination: the boy can smile, whistle and stand on one foot, and he walks in a straight line; all appears to be normal. I note from the corner of my eye that his father is absorbed in reading the newspaper that someone left on the seats.

I ask Bill to put his shoes back on and suddenly Phillip, who is still waiting to speak to me, touches my hand, his eyes looking down at the boy who is in the process of putting his shoes back on.

Bill struggles to lace his school shoes: no matter how many times he tries, he cannot do the knot. We look at each other and have the same thought: this is serious. The boy cannot respond to his brain commands and control his hands' movements. We need an urgent x-ray of the skull and a neurological opinion. I whisper to Phillip, asking if he could speak to the father and shake him out of his indifference.

42
FIRST HOME

Looking for a house is not easy when the income is limited. Bromley, Sevenoaks and Petts Wood have lovely houses but they are beyond our means. We find, after a lot of searching and visits, a reasonably priced house in Sidcup. It has three bedrooms, a through lounge and a garage too narrow to allow a car to be parked in there. But, it's good for storing things.

The journey to our house takes about 35 minutes. All I have to do is take the Underground from Southwark Bridge station to London Bridge and then join the suburban train from London Bridge to Sidcup. The train carriage has at least six sets of doors on both sides, each serving every compartment, which open manually and close with a loud bang. At main stations, when lots of people descend, there is a true symphony of banging doors. As the doors are on either side of the carriage, one has to be careful which side the platform is so as not to end up on the wrong side with live lines. I can see my house in the distance and wish that the train would stop there, at my back garden, to save me the ten-minute walk from New Eltham station. When I am not tired, it is all right, as the streets I pass are lined with Japanese cherry trees; their bark is mahogany red and the flowers are deep rose when in bloom. On passing, I look in at the different gardens and appreciate the flowers and bushes, and the colour of the front doors, as well as the window frames. Otherwise, one could be left lost and bewildered in the uniformity of the rows of semi-detached houses that were built between the wars. Almost all of them were built on two levels and pebble-dashed outside. One of those houses is ours and I recognise it by the tall Japanese cherry trees planted by previous owners in the front garden. We have three bedrooms because the previous owner built an extension above the garage. We have a long, narrow garden set with an oblong lawn, bordered by a few rose bushes. We hear the trains behind rattling by. Saying that the house is ours is not entirely accurate, asit was bought with a mortgage. Everything we have is only partly ours: furniture, kitchen utensils and even clothes. Every month we chip at the wall of money to add a grain to our own walls.

A year or so later, Dan is made redundant. Ray, the owner of the company, is made to choose between the foreman and his team of workers, and Dan, the foreigner with new ideas of management. Ray chooses the workers and their foreman: he can't afford to lose them in the troubled economic times. Overnight people from the factory come to our house and demand the keys to remove the company car. Dan is upset; he starts again the tedious process of finding a job. We are both irritable and snappy. Money is scarce.

We never experienced redundancy in Romania; employment was granted for a working life, unless some catastrophic event changed that. We earned little, barely enough to keep ourselves alive, but come the first day of the month or the 15th, we got our pay. So here we are, with the half-salary that I earn, the mortgage and Nicky's school fees; we are in trouble.

Nicky is at home with us. As soon as we settled in our house, she couldn't wait to be back. But Dan insisted that she should go to a private school so she joined the senior school in Bromley. The savings that Dan has set aside from his French employment dwindle fast. It takes another eight or nine months till he finds another job and this time in his specialty: the oil industry. That means he has to travel abroad a great deal of the time.

Strikes continue on and off. Some days there is no electricity and no light. And it is raining heavily almost every day. There are train strikes and the journey to London Bridge is by bus, if the bus is not full. The traffic is at a standstill; the roads are packed with cars, and so it takes hours to get from A to B. There is a call from the Councils and the Government asking everyone who has a car to take the stranded commuters to work. Guy's hospital administrators take a very rigid attitude: we have to be at work on time; any time off will be deducted from our holiday. One day, the bread companies' workers go on strike. The previous days, people rushed to the shops to stock up on bread. Dan is away and I haven't got the time. We have flour and I attempt to make bread, which I've never made before. The loaves come out heavy as a brick. When Dan returns, he and Nicky play a game of catch with my loaves. Only our dog, Brandy, enjoys them.

The rain continues to fall relentlessly and we discover that our street is prone to flooding. Sandbags are distributed from the local council. With anxiety, we watch the water level rising. The street and the front garden flood but the water stops at the garage door. On such a morning, very early, I hear the doorbell ringing. A group of people stand by the gate and I recognise some faces under the hoods. They all wear raincoats and wellies. They want to know if we are all right and whether we need anything. They go on and knock at every door. Such kindness lifts my spirits from the gloom.

Then the sun comes out and we start again, tidying up, tending the gardens. The good thing is that we get friendlier with our neighbours. The elderly lady on our right comes out for a chat across the fence, and the brother and sister in the adjoining house on our left acknowledge us and advise me on how to save some of the plants. The saying that every cloud has a silver lining begins to ring true.

I receive news that my parents have been given permission to leave Romania and go to Israel. Finally, they could endure the Ceausescu's harsh regime no more.

I fly to Israel to greet them. The year is 1974. The reunion with Mady and Uncle Abraham is very emotional, and seeing them fills me with joy as well as some regrets. My sister Bea joins me and together we go to the airport on the day of our parents' arrival. There is a crowd waiting and the police try to keep us back. The group of immigrants have arrived; they have to be processed, registered and allocated to different places round the country. I spot my mother looking through the window, her anxious eyes behind the glasses, searching. I push my way through the crowd to get as near as possible. I cannot see my sister in the crowd to tell her. I have not seen my mother for more than six years. She looks the same: only her hair has turned grey. We make eye contact and then I see her mouthing the words: 'Where is Bea?'

I answer that Bea is here - I'll go and fetch her. With that she turns around; she seems happy with that. I see them later; they settle in Hedera. My father is so happy to see my sister and me. A few days later I say goodbye and take a flight back home. On the way back I cannot stop thinking: *What if I stayed on?*

43
PASS

I put in an application for an exam DCH or diploma in child health. I pay more than two months' salary for the fees and just before Christmas I sit the exam. A few weeks of waiting and I just scrape though. Time to start seriously thinking about my main exams. The new paediatrics department is almost ready in Guy's and the tower block is dominating the skyscape. Evelina will be closed soon and we will move into the new Children's Unit at Guy's. It is a lovely airy luminous building with plenty of seating, a television and lots of toys to amuse the children while they wait. We had a television in the doctors' room at the old Evelina but we came in one day to find that it had been stolen, by whom we never found out. I have been offered another contract - this time for one year.

My appointment extends to one year, then two and then three.

I walk down Harley Street towards Trafalgar Square and on to Charring Cross train station. The pulse is beating against my temples: 1-2, 1-2 pass. Pass. Tears are rolling down my face. 'Can't be that bad! Cheer up! Tomorrow will be better,' someone says in passing.

What is he talking about? Little does he know that these are tears of joy. I've passed my exam! I've finally passed it. In a fit of adrenaline rush at the end of my vivas, sensing victory, I stood up and shook hands with the astounded examiners.

It is drizzly and grey, and on the street people are pushing this way and that, but it doesn't matter! I passed! 1-2, 1-2.

The woolly scarf which I pull over my head to protect me from the rain gets heavier as it absorbs more water. The train arrives on time; this is a miracle because there is a strike on. The previous trains were cancelled so the crowd surges forward and I stand all the way to New Eltham squeezed between two men, their open newspapers almost covering my head. I walk the back streets till I reach the postbox on the corner of Brooklands Avenue. Some rose bushes still have blooms on empty prickly twigs and sandbags are still visible in front of entrances, remnants from the recent flood. Any heavy rain floods our street. I greet the neighbours who happen to be outside with a smile. Till recently nobody paid any attention to our greetings - till the day when someone noticed us in the garden, tending the roses. Someone stopped, said hello and admired our roses. Since then we are on nodding terms and exchange the odd greeting with most of our neighbours. This time they smile back, not knowing how happy I am. I reach home almost running, ready to give my news.

'Mammy, I am going out with Lizy.' Nicky's voice greets me from the top landing.

'All right,' I reply, smiling.

Dan is out at work. I am to enjoy the moment by myself. Pass! Pass, 1-2, 1-2.

We settle down. I feel more adjusted and we are slightly more in tune with each other. Nicky is settled at school; she is a senior in the lower school now. She loves to go to school, see her friends and bring them to visit. She goes to parties. Parents come to drop their children off and then come to fetch them home. Dan and I ask them in for a cup of tea and sometimes we have a little chat. Nice people. One day, one of the mothers suggests that she could give Nicky a lift to school, as I don't drive. Her name is Win and we become friends.

London remains unsettled because of the Irish threats. One lunchtime I arrive and I am greeted by an atmosphere of anxiety. A bomb was thrown at the Tower of London; Dutch children on holiday were caught in the blast while visiting the Crown Jewels and we are expecting casualties. The whole hospital is on alert. In the event, they are brought directly to the main hospital and the surgeons are already at work. I am thinking: *it could have been us; it could have been Nicky.*

44
EPILOGUE

We are British! It is official! The year is 1976 and I am pregnant. The certificate of naturalisation confirms our new status. By now I feel that I am part of this country. We are husband and wife; we have one child together and another is growing inside me. 'English fresh air,' my friends say. We can start looking forward to living our lives: travelling to new parts of the world, reading the books we want, enjoying the work I do, seeing friends I love and saying whatever I have to say.

One settles in a new life like one settles into a new pair of shoes: at the beginning one craves to have them and then one starts wearing them. They hurt a little and they rub a little but in time they give and one gets used to them. After a while they are the only shoes one wants to wear and be comfortable in. But they wear out and holes appear.

We are together, we have our home and I enjoy working in my practice. Nicky is growing into a lovely, well-accomplished young woman. We go to concerts and theatres. We start travelling and visit other countries. At least, I do. Dan has discovered a fear of flying so, unless he travels on business, he does not travel at all. He hates holidays and even when persuaded to take time off, he never parts from the telephone. Only in the peace and stability do we realise how far apart we have travelled.

Dan is intent on making money, on striking it rich. But his goal is hard to achieve. He is not born to money, and is naturally inclined towards research and study. He has no entrepreneurial skills. In time he will achieve a forum for Romanian and British business, the Chamber of Commerce. Rubbing shoulders with ministers, heads of industry and foreign diplomats is more what he enjoys. In the meantime, I find satisfaction in stability, friends, my patients, my practice and my new baby girl - fragile and tough, as any premature baby is.

What we started together begins to unravel. We limp together through years of stability and better quality of life. We move into a larger house with a bigger garden and Dan travels to and fro in his car; we see very little of each other. Years flow by.

This morning the sun is shining, although the forecast is showers in the afternoon. I can just about see the cumuli gathering grey in the distant sky.

Above me the sun is shining and the air is milk. I am out in the garden, tending the roses. This is something that my mother used to do after the war but at the time I did not pay attention. My work, which I enjoy, takes me to several baby clinics and to the practice I joined; my two other partners are like brothers to me. I have a good nanny who looks after my baby. Dan and I are together but I feel it in my bones that it is not going to last for long. We've achieved what we wanted to do, and now? He remains restless and searching. He won't leave me, not till he finds someone else to prop him up and fit in with his plans, whatever those may be. And I must say, I don't even mind it. For now we will try to work at it: perhaps this new baby will bring us close or perhaps we'll drift into old age like so many other couples, each one on their own.

Biography

Miry Vicks started writing fiction after her retirement. She was a family general medical practitioner for more than 40 years. She lives in Brighton .She has two daughters and two grandchildren. Her life took her from her place of birth in Romania, to Israel, France and England. Miry started writing her memoir at the suggestion of her granddaughter. The younger generation felt that Miry's pathway through life was miles apart from the lives of her daughters and grand children. Her first book, 'Myra the silent child who found a voice' was self-published on Amazon Kindle in January 2013.

'Immigration Masterclass' is her second book.

Lightning Source UK Ltd.
Milton Keynes UK
UKOW06f0859040116
265729UK00019B/776/P

9 781849 148221